access to history

POVERTY
and WELFARE
1830–1914

access to history

POVERTY *and* WELFARE 1830–1914

Peter Murray

Hodder & Stoughton

A MEMBER OF THE HODDER HEADLINE GROUP

The publishers would like to thank the following for permission to reproduce material in this volume: Fontana for an extract from *The Rise of Respectable Society* by F.M.L. Thompson (1989); Manchester University Press for an extract from *Exiles of Erin* by Lynn Lees (1979); Macmillan for extracts from 'The Wealth of Nations' by Adam Smith quoted in *The Relief of Poverty 1834-1914* by M.E. Rose (1972) and *The Evolution of the British Welfare State* by Frazer (2nd edition, 1984); Pelican for an extract from *Industry and Empire* by Eric Hobsbawm (1968); Rivers Oram for an extract from *Women in Hackney* by Anna Davin (1996); Routledge for an extract from *Social History of England* by Francois Bedarida (1991); Virago for extracts from *Round About A Pound A Week* by Maud Pember Reeves (1979); Routledge for extracts from *Idle Hands, The Experience of Unemployment* by John Burnett (ed.) (1994).

The publishers would like to thank the following for permission to reproduce material in this volume: The Illustrated London News Picture Library page 40, page 108; Public Record Office page 43, page 46, page 67, page 72, page 101.

Orders: please contact Bookpoint Ltd, 39 Milton Park, Abingdon, Oxon OX14 4TD. Telephone: (44) 01235 400414, Fax: (44) 01235 400454. Lines are open from 9.00 - 6.00, Monday to Saturday, with a 24 hour message answering service. Email address: orders@bookpoint.co.uk

British Library Cataloguing in Publication Data

A catalogue for this title is available from the British Library

ISBN 0 340 61891 4

First published 1999

Impression number	10	9	8	7	6	5	4	3	2	1
Year			2004	2003	2002	2001	2000	1999		

The cover illustration is entitled 'Applicants for admission to a casual ward' reproduced by courtesy of the Bridgeman Art Library.

Typeset by Sempringham publishing services, Bedford
Printed in Great Britain for Hodder & Stoughton Educational,
a division of Hodder Headline Plc, 338 Euston Road, London NW1 3BH
by Redwood Books, Trowbridge, Wiltshire.

Contents

Preface

To the general reader

Although the *Access to History* series has been designed with the needs of students studying the subject at higher examination levels very much in mind, it also has a great deal to offer the general reader. The main body of the text (i.e. ignoring the 'Study Guides' at the ends of chapters) forms a readable and yet stimulating survey of a coherent topic as studied by historians. However, each author's aim has not merely been to provide a clear explanation of what happened in the past (to interest and inform): it has also been assumed that most readers wish to be stimulated into thinking further about the topic and to form opinions of their own about the significance of the events that are described and discussed (to be challenged). Thus, although no prior knowledge of the topic is expected on the reader's part, she or he is treated as an intelligent and thinking person throughout. The author tends to share ideas and possibilities with the reader, rather than passing on numbers of so-called 'historical truths'.

To the student reader

There are many ways in which the series can be used by students studying history at a higher level. It will, therefore, be worthwhile thinking about your own study strategy before you start your work on this book. Obviously, your strategy will vary depending on the aim you have in mind, and the time for study that is available to you.

If, for example, you want to acquire a general overview of the topic in the shortest possible time, the following approach will probably be the most effective:

1. Read Chapter 1 and think about its contents.
2. Read the 'Working On ...' sections at the end of Chapter 2 and decide whether it is necessary for you to read this chapter.
3. If it is, read the chapter, stopping at each heading to note down the main points that have been made.
4. Repeat stage 2 (and stage 3 where appropriate) for all the other chapters.

If, however, your aim is to gain a thorough grasp of the topic, taking however much time is necessary to do so, you may benefit from carrying out the same procedure with each chapter, as follows:

1. Read the chapter as fast as you can, and preferably at one sitting.
2. Study the summary diagram at the end of the chapter, ensuring that you understand the general 'shape' of what you have just read.

3. Read the 'Working On ...' sections (and the 'Answering essay questions' section, if there is one) and decide what further work you need to do on the chapter. In particularly important sections of the book, this will involve reading the chapter a second time and stopping at each heading to think about (and to write a summary of) what you have just read.
4. Attempt the 'Source-based questions' section. It will sometimes be sufficient to think through your answers, but additional understanding will often be gained by forcing yourself to write them down.

When you have finished the main chapters of the book, study the 'Further Reading' section and decide what additional reading (if any) you will do on the topic.

This book has been designed to help make your studies both enjoyable and successful. If you can think of ways in which this could have been done more effectively, please write to tell me. In the meantime, I hope that you will gain greatly from your study of History.

Keith Randell

1 Introduction: Poverty and the Poor

'POINTS TO CONSIDER

This chapter will introduce you to some of the key concepts used in the study of poverty and welfare. It will also give you an initial impression of who the poor were and what it was like to be poor in the nineteenth and early twentieth centuries. Your aim on first reading the chapter should be to understand the key terms and concepts which will be used throughout this book and to develop a picture of what poverty meant in this period.

KEY DATES

1776   Adam Smith's *Wealth of Nations* published. Includes definition of 'relative' poverty.

1834   Poor Law Amendment Act. Major Act of Parliament which reorganised the Poor Law in England and Wales.

1851-52 Henry Mayhew's *London Labour and the London Poor* first published in serial form. The first extensive study to look at poverty in London in this period.

1878   'General' William Booth founds the Salvation Army: an attempt to bring Christianity to the poor.

1908   Old Age Pensions Act. State pensions introduced for elderly citizens by the Liberal Government.

1 Introduction: The Nineteenth Century Context

KEY ISSUE What were the main social and economic developments which dominated nineteenth-century history?

By 1830 Britain was experiencing a period of profound social and economic change. The 'industrial revolution' had witnessed the application of powered machinery to the manufacturing process. Small-scale textile production in the home was replaced, increasingly, by large-scale production in factories. Manufacturers were able to make large profits because of the efficiency of the factory system. New towns grew up as workers were both attracted from the countryside by the prospect of higher earnings and greater independence, and forced out of agriculture by the dual forces of mechanisation and land enclosure. Although the majority of the population still lived in the countryside in 1830, by the time of the 1851 Census just over half the population of England and Wales were living in towns or cities: the world's first industrial nation had become the world's first urbanised society.

The titanic forces of industrialisation and urbanisation had many consequences. Natural forces like the weather had always led to poverty and distress in agriculture. To these were now added the unpredictable swings in trade that characterised the early industrial economy. Technological change could destroy jobs as well as create them. Although poverty was not a new phenomenon, the concentration of the industrial poor in overcrowded towns made poverty both more visible and more terrifying to those with wealth and authority in society. As the problem of poverty became more obvious, the need for new solutions to the problem became pressing.

2 Poverty and Welfare: Some Key Concepts

> **KEY ISSUES** What are the different ways of categorising poverty and the poor? What are meant by collectivist, individualist, central and local solutions to the problem of poverty?

a) Absolute and Relative Poverty

Poverty can be defined in two ways. When we see pictures of people starving to death as a result of famine or disaster we are in no doubt that they are poor. The lack of an adequate income to provide for basic human needs - food, clothing, warmth and shelter - is a clear indication of poverty. Such a condition is often termed *absolute poverty*. People are in absolute poverty because they cannot gain access to basic necessities, no matter how they organise their resources. Absolute poverty is still widespread at the start of the twenty-first century, although it is rare in the more industrialised and technologically advanced societies. However, this does not mean that poverty is absent in these societies.

Another way of defining poverty is to look at it in a relative way. In the first half of the nineteenth century the advances in agricultural production meant that famine as a result of crop failure in Great Britain (though not in Ireland) had become a thing of the past. But there was general agreement that poverty had not been conquered. Many people, especially those who were forced out of employment by the monumental changes of the industrial revolution, were absolutely poor. Others, however, might still be thought of as being poor even though they were able to gain access to the basic necessities of life. There was an assumption that a certain standard of living was normal, and that those living below this, while they might not be starving or homeless, were certainly poor. Adam Smith, the pioneering economist of the late 1700s, agreed that poverty was the absence of the necessities of life, but he defined these as,

> not only the commodities which are indispensably necessary for the support of life, but whatever the custom of the country renders it indecent for creditable people, even of the lowest order, to be without.

In Britain and Ireland during the period 1830-1914 there were people who were absolutely poor, but there were many more who were relatively poor. Both concepts need to be kept in mind in any investigation of poverty and the attempts to respond to it.

b) The Deserving and the Undeserving

The link between poverty and morality is very important in understanding the way in which people in the nineteenth and early twentieth centuries looked at the poor. Many observers and investigators of poverty claimed that the poor were often responsible for their own misery. Carelessness, laziness and drunkenness, it was said, were the real causes of poverty. People who were poor as a result of their moral failures were regarded as undeserving; they might be given some help, but this would be of the meanest kind, designed to punish them for their inadequacies and to encourage them to mend their ways. On the other hand, it was acknowledged that some people, though they lived honest and hardworking lives, might find themselves plunged into poverty as a result of circumstances beyond their control. These were the deserving poor, the poor who had a greater moral claim to support in time of need.

Charity workers, welfare authorities, politicians and writers were often obsessed with the need to distinguish the deserving from the undeserving. Their great fear was that too generous a support for the poor would encourage immoral behaviour and reduce the incentive to lead a responsible and independent life. The issue of unemployment highlighted this problem. If those without work were given financial help why, it was asked, should anyone bother to work? Such a view inevitably led to a search for effective ways to provide support whilst discouraging dependence on the State, or pauperism (a pauper was someone in receipt of Poor Law payments). For those responsible for providing welfare to those in need, the Poor Law authorities, this meant (after 1834) subjecting the poor who asked for help to the harshest of regimes (see Chapter 3). This, it was believed, would encourage anyone who could to avoid the Poor Law altogether and lead an independent life. But what of the deserving poor? Why should those who were unemployed due to a trade depression, for example, be punished as if they had done something wrong? This was the dilemma facing welfare reformers throughout this period, and the problem facing those who found themselves in need of help.

c) Ways of Providing Welfare

Any society has a number of choices as to the way it provides welfare for its members. Put simply, welfare can be provided either by government, by organisations which are independent of government, or it can be left to individuals. If government itself provides welfare, it can either do this centrally or through local government.

Welfare systems provided by government are known as collectivist solutions. Society collectively, through its government and laws, decides that help must be given to those in need. Collectivist solutions to poverty provided by government have certain features often seen as desirable in welfare systems. Firstly, there is a stronger guarantee that they will not break down than is the case with alternative systems. Although it is possible for government welfare systems to collapse when a country enters a period of crisis, the relatively stable political system in modern Britain has given its citizens a degree of confidence in government welfare provision. However inadequate the system might seem, it is unlikely to break down altogether. Secondly, government welfare systems are backed by law, which again gives them an inherent strength. Finally, government welfare tends to involve a certain amount of wealth redistribution. Richer sections of the community pay higher taxes which are then transferred to the poorer sections through welfare benefits. Of course, government welfare systems are not necessarily redistributive, but they do tend in that direction.

The relationship between national government and local government is an important feature of welfare in this period. The major collectivist government welfare system in the nineteenth century was the Poor Law (see Chapters 2 and 3). The Poor Law, reorganised by an amending Act in 1834, was a national, state system in that it covered the whole country and the administration was supervised by government officials in London. Nevertheless, the system was financed through local taxes, organised through groups of local parishes known as Unions and operated by bodies of locally elected representatives known as Guardians. Such a system grew out of the tradition of local government responsibility for the poor which had existed for hundreds of years. But because different areas had varying levels of poverty and wealth, inequalities inevitably resulted. This led to a demand for nationally administered welfare systems. However, even when the Liberal Government brought in national, government-financed old age pensions in 1908 (see Chapter 6), they still relied on local committees to decide who was eligible for the benefits.

Governments are not the only institutions capable of providing collectivist solutions. In the nineteenth century, friendly societies and trade unions were formed when groups of people collectively joined together to provide mutual support for one another in time of need. The members of these organisations chose to pool some of their resources by way of subscriptions so as to provide themselves with help should they need it at a future date. Voluntary organisations like these could be very successful, and in the nineteenth century they provided welfare for millions of working people. However, the cost of subscriptions excluded many of those who were most in need and the organisations were also prone to financial difficulties or even complete collapse. They had neither the financial resources nor the legal power of the State, even though governments did pass laws to regulate the operation of both friendly societies and trade unions. (See Chapter 4)

Individualist responses to poverty are those which put individual responsibility at the centre of welfare provision. At one extreme, this could be the attitude that all individuals either sink or swim and should expect no help in time of crisis. It is up to them, according to this view, to save money in the good times to provide for themselves in the bad times. The nineteenth-century doctrine of 'self-help' put this type of attitude at the heart of its philosophy. However, self-help also recognised that individualism could work through collective organisations. Private insurance companies provided prudent individuals with a mechanism for protecting themselves against future disaster. Charities, especially those that operated under the guidance of the Charity Organisation Society (an organisation which attempted to limit charitable giving to the 'deserving' only), gave a little help to those in need primarily in order to help them become self-supporting individuals. Indeed, both the Poor Law and the friendly societies also sought to encourage the poor to stand on their own feet. Thus, in a strange way collectivist systems of welfare might well operate under individualist principles.

3 Who Were the Poor?

> **KEY ISSUE** What were the different definitions of 'the poor' in the period 1832-1914? Did 'the poor' form a clearly defined or a fluctuating group?

When nineteenth-century commentators wrote about 'the poor' they were referring to any one of a range of different groupings within society. In the widest sense, all those who existed by virtue of their physical or mental efforts alone could be regarded as poor. Sometimes this group was referred to as the 'working class' or 'working classes', sometimes as 'the lower orders' or 'the labouring poor', sometimes as 'the proletariat', or even as 'the people'. For many historians, the exact classification is of great significance. In his book *The Making of the English Working Class*, E.P. Thompson argued that the industrial revolution produced a single working class which was conscious of its own status and identity.[1] This, he believed, was a new and unprecedented development, full of importance for the future progress of society. Other historians have preferred to highlight the distinctions between different groups of workers and have disputed the existence of a united working class. They prefer to use looser terms to describe the mass of the population. For example, it is the view of the French historian Francois Bedarida that,

1 the lumping together under the heading of 'proletariat' of such varied
    social groups as factory hands, artisans and craftsmen, small-scale
    employers, tradesmen, subcontractors, farm labourers and domestic
    servants, leads to an excessive simplification which in the end is hardly
5 illuminating. Doubtless all these categories had certain things in
    common: the dependence on the owners of capital, the same insecurity,
    the same low incomes; but they differed so much in other aspects - way
    of life, relation with their employers, leisure activities, culture, family life,
    neighbourhood relations, religious beliefs - that one would do better to
10 combine them in a larger ensemble with a genuine collective conscious-
    ness, that is as the popular classes.[2]

Whatever the distinctions or classifications, it is clear that the
working class or 'popular classes' were poor relative to those who
controlled the Nation's wealth and property. At the end of the period
covered by this book, one estimate suggests that the richest 1 per
cent of the population owned 67 per cent of the Nation's wealth
while the bottom 87 per cent of the population shared a mere 8 per
cent of the wealth. While this does not mean that the majority of the
population lived in permanent absolute poverty, it does help to
explain why the majority of the population lived in fear of poverty:
they had little surplus wealth to call on in time of need. With few
financial resources to fall back on, any sudden disaster such as illness,
death or unemployment could plunge a family into poverty.

The relationship between poverty, the wider working class and the
core of people in permanent poverty was well illustrated by 'General'
William Booth, the founder of the Salvation Army. Writing in 1890,
Booth was also one of those who was keen to distinguish between the
deserving and the undeserving, even if he and his organisation were
prepared to spend much of their time on the latter. But Booth understood that poverty was not simply a matter of moral failure:

1 Darkest England may be described as consisting broadly of three circles,
    one within the other. The outer and widest circle is inhabited by the
    starving and homeless, but honest Poor. The second by those who live
    by Vice; and the third and innermost region at the centre is peopled by
5 those who exist by Crime. The whole of the three circles is sodden with
    drink. ... The borders of this great lost land are not sharply defined. They
    are continually expanding and contracting. Whenever there is a period
    of depression in trade, they stretch; when prosperity returns, they
    contract. So far as individuals are concerned, there are none among the
10 hundreds of thousands who live upon the outskirts of the dark forest
    who can truly say that they or their children are secure from being
    hopelessly entangled in its labyrinth. The death of a breadwinner, a long
    illness, a failure in the city, or any one of a thousand other causes which
    might be named, will bring within the first circle those who at present
15 imagine themselves free from all danger of actual want.

Beyond the outer edge of William Booth's first circle lay the skilled workers in permanent employment. A great deal has been written about the distinction between these relatively prosperous skilled workers - sometimes known as the labour aristocracy - and the mass of unskilled workers. Whilst the skilled and relatively prosperous workers could afford to make some provision for the future, they too were vulnerable to poverty resulting from some crisis. In the early nineteenth century the clearest example of this was the case of the handloom weavers: skilled textile workers who wove cloth for sale to merchants or clothes-makers. Thriving in the early 1800s, the hand-loom weavers found that they were unable to compete with the new textile factories. Despite their high level of skill, the handloom weavers were gradually reduced to a state of misery as their earnings collapsed even though they worked longer and longer hours. Technological change could destroy the prosperity of even the most skilled of the working classes.

If even prospering workers could find themselves suddenly facing poverty, then one can imagine how large the spectre of poverty loomed in the lives of those on lower incomes, those at the edge of Booth's first circle. Insecurity and fear were dominant themes in the lives of working people throughout this period. Temporary poverty was likely, at some time, to affect the majority of the population, and this could easily lead to permanent poverty. It only took one crisis, one decision by an employer, one accident, and people could find their lives transformed from minimal comfort to wretched misery. When 'the thing', as the American writer Jack London described it, happened, life might never be the same again. The circumstances which could draw an individual into the inner circles of poverty were illustrated by the story of 'Ginger', a man London met in the queue for the casual ward of the Whitechapel workhouse, which was known as 'the Spike':

1   A year before, one day, while in the employ of a fish dealer, he was carrying a heavy box of fish which was too much for him. Result: 'something broke', and there was the box on the ground, and he on the ground beside it.

5   At the first hospital, whither he was immediately carried, they said it was a rupture, reduced the swelling, gave him some Vaseline to rub on it, kept him four hours, and told him to get along. But he was not on the streets more than two or three hours when he was down on his back again. This time he went to another hospital and was patched up. But the

10   point is, the employer did nothing, positively nothing, for the man injured in his employment, and even refused him 'a light job now and again', when he came out. As far as Ginger is concerned, he is a broken man. His only chance to earn a living was by heavy work. He is now incapable of performing heavy work, and from now until he dies, the spike, the peg,

15   and the streets are all he can look forward to in the way of food and shelter. The thing happened - that is all. He put his back under too great

a load of fish, and his chance for happiness in life was crossed off the books.

A narrower conception of the poor in this period limited those in this category to a more tightly drawn circle than the working class as a whole. Many nineteenth-century observers who ventured into the worst urban slums of industrial England detected a population at the bottom of society whose miserable lives were entirely shaped by the poverty in which they existed. Many of these people had sunk to the lowest level of existence as a result of some catastrophe in their lives, whilst others were born into an environment of deprivation, low wages and lack of opportunity. These were the inhabitants of William Booth's inner circles of 'Darkest England'. Writers often referred to this population as if they were a separate race, an undiscovered country, a people set apart from civilised society. In his *Report on the Sanitary Condition of the Labouring Population of Great Britain* in 1842, the poor law administrator and health reformer, Edwin Chadwick, was one of the first to describe the poorest areas as an 'unknown country'. Henry Mayhew, describing the 'street-folk' of London in the 1850s, wrote of 'unknown regions' which contained 'strange tribes of men'. Throughout the period writers continued to discuss the poorest sections of the population in these terms. They were the outcasts, the residuum, the 'people of the abyss'. When Charles Booth in the late nineteenth century and Seebohm Rowntree at the start of the twentieth century conducted their surveys of poverty (see Chapter 5), they too recognised a very poor class at the foot of the social ladder. Rowntree defined the really poor in York as those who existed below his poverty line, a level beneath which families did not have enough money to maintain 'mere physical efficiency' - they did not have enough to live on.

In one sense there was a justification in distinguishing the plight of the very poor from that of the wider working class. 'Respectable' workers, employed in steady, skilled occupations and living away from the slums and 'rookeries' of the inner cities, themselves emphasised their difference from the poorer workers. Writing in 1873, Thomas Wright, a skilled engineer, explained that while the craftsman,

> ... resents the spirit in which the followers of 'genteel occupations' look down on him, he in his turn looks down upon the labourer. The artisan creed with regard to labourers is that the latter are an inferior class, and that they should be made to know and kept in their place.

On the other hand, as with the case of the handloom weavers, even the most respectable and skilled of workers might find themselves drawn down into a more humble position, and into the poverty that went with such a fall.

4 The Experience of Poverty

> **KEY ISSUE** What was it like to be poor in Victorian or Edwardian England? What did poverty mean in terms of living standards?

The experience of poverty affected all aspects of life. At various points in the period, writers attempted to describe the reality of poverty in financial terms. The currency of the period consisted of pounds, shillings and pence (often known as 'pennies'). Each pound was subdivided into 20 shillings, and each shilling was made up of 12 pence. Pennies could themselves be divided up into halfpennies and farthings (a farthing was a quarter of a penny). Although there was some variation in the level of wages and prices at various points in the period 1832-1914, inflation (the term for a general rise in the level of prices) over the whole period was not significant. It is therefore unsurprising that commentators were consistent in the minimum level of income they identified as being necessary for survival throughout the period. Roughly speaking, this level, for a small family, was about £1 per week. A single person could live on less. The consequences of not managing to make do with a small income were explained memorably by Charles Dickens' character Mr Micawber:

> 1 My other piece of advice, Copperfield,' said Mr Micawber, 'you know. Annual income twenty pounds, annual expenditure nineteen nineteen six [nineteen pounds, nineteen shillings and six pennies], result happiness. Annual income twenty pounds, annual expenditure twenty pounds
> 5 ought and six, result misery. The blossom is blighted, the leaf is withered, the God of day goes down upon the dreary scene, and - and in short you are forever floored. As I am!

Fifty years later, Seebohm Rowntree set the precise boundary between misery and happiness for a family of five (husband, wife and three children) at 21s 8d (one pound one shilling and eight pence) per week. The reality of survival on such a tight budget was described by Jack London:

Rent	6s. 0d.	Oil	8d.
Bread	4s. 0d.	Sugar	9d.
Meat	3s. 6d.	Milk	6d.
Vegetables	2s. 6d.	Soap	4d.
Coals	1s. 0d.	Butter	10d.
Tea	9d.	Firewood	4d.
			21s. 2d.

> 1 ... While the table given above will permit no extravagance, no overloading of stomachs, it will be noticed that there is no surplus. The whole

guinea is spent for food and rent. There is no pocket money left over.
Does the man buy a glass of beer, the family must eat that much less;
5 and in so far as it eats less, just that far will it impair its physical efficiency. The members of this family cannot ride in buses or trams, cannot
write letters, take outings, go to a 'tu'penny gaff' for cheap vaudeville,
join social or benefit clubs, nor can they buy sweetmeats, tobacco, books
or newspapers. And further, should one child (and there are three)
10 require a pair of shoes, the family must strike meat for a week from its
bill of fare ...

The diets of those operating on or below such a budget were
inevitably limited and it took great ingenuity on the part of the housewife to both provide sufficient meals and avoid monotony. Household
management skills were also put to the test when attempting to
organise living and sleeping arrangements in often cramped and
inadequate accommodation. Between 1909 and 1913 Maud Pember
Reeves of the Fabian Women's Group conducted a survey of working-
class conditions in a 'respectable' district in Lambeth, south London.
The conditions endured are illustrated by one example of a family
inhabiting a single 15 feet by 13 feet room:

1 Under the window facing the door is the large bed, in which sleep
mother, father and two children. A perambulator by the bedside
accommodates the baby, and in the further corner is a small cot for
the remaining child. The second window can be, and is, left partly open
5 at night. At the foot of the bed which crosses the window is a small
square table. Three wooden chairs and a chest of drawers complete
the furniture ... The small fireplace has no oven, and open shelves go
up each side of it. There are two saucepans, both burnt. There is no
larder.

Some people at this level of society had slightly better conditions,
but many endured a lot worse. As with food and indeed all the
other aspects of life, lack of money meant lack of choice, and the
Victorian and Edwardian poor had to do the best they could
on the resources they had. Sometimes, particularly as a result of
unemployment, sickness or old age, these resources simply were not
enough. It was at these points that the poor were forced to look to
friends, charities, institutions like the friendly societies or the State
itself for welfare support. The extent to which this support
succeeded in alleviating the poverty of the poor is perhaps the
central question in the history of poverty and welfare in this
period.

References

1   E.P. Thompson, *The Making of the English Working Class* (Pantheon, 1964).
2   F. Bedarida, *A Social History of England 1851-1990* (Routledge ed., 1991)
    p. 59.

Working on Chapter 1

The concepts introduced in the first section of this chapter are important to understand, so you will need to write out your own brief definition of each. One way of making notes on the second section might be to construct a diagram based on concentric circles, as suggested in the extract from William Booth. The last section is intended to give you a sense of what poverty really meant. It would be useful to draw up a list of all the elements that went with 'being poor' based on this section.

Source-based questions on Chapter 1

Certain types of source-based questions appear regularly on exam papers. In this first group of questions the focus of each question is indicated in brackets after each question. You will need to make your own judgement on the question focus in subsequent chapters, but you can refer back to the following guidance for help.

Comprehension. Comprehension questions are the most straightforward type of source-based questions you are likely to face. These questions require you to extract a specific piece of information from the source, or to explain what the author means by a particular reference, word or phrase. They may well begin with the word 'explain' or with the phrase 'what does author X mean … ?'. Such questions are testing your ability to comprehend the meaning of a source. The most important thing is to be clear, to focus on the *specific* information requested, and to avoid including information that is irrelevant or giving over-long explanations.

Comparison. Comparison questions will cover two or more extracts. The question requires you to compare two sources, normally with regard to a specific issue. For example, 'To what extent does the author of extract A support the views of author B on issue C?'. You must focus on the *specific issue*. Do not be side-tracked into comparisons over other issues which are not asked about in the question. If the question begins with the phrases 'To what extent …' or 'How far …', you must give both sides of the argument. In other words, you must explain the ways in which they *do agree* and the ways in which they *do not agree*. You will then need to weigh up the two arguments and make a clear judgement: are the extracts *mainly in agreement* or do they *mainly disagree*?

Source Reliability. This type of question focuses on the nature and origins of a specific extract. Some sources have innate qualities and weaknesses which historians must bare in mind when using them. For example, an autobiography is very useful in that it is a person's own recollections and they may well be unique. On the other hand, if it is written a long time after the event in question it may be unreliable either because the individual's memory has failed or because they

Summary Diagram
Introduction: Poverty and the Poor

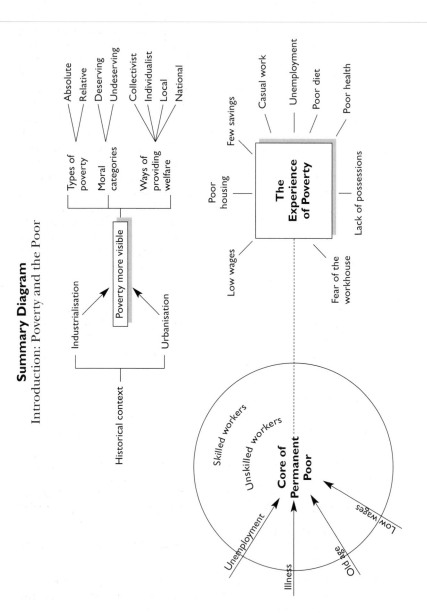

may wish to portray their role in a favourable light. Questions might also ask you to look at the *language and tone* of an extract. The aim of this is to determine whether the *style* an author uses provides a clue as to their point of view. Look for repeated phrases, dramatic accounts and the frequent use of adjectives. These are all devices which may indicate that the author is committed to a particular point of view which they want others to share.

All sources must be examined to discover the *motivation* of their authors and the *reliability* of their information. Look for the clues. *Who* produced the extract, *why* and *for* whom was it intended? The writer/speaker may have a particular reason to present things to suit their opinion or to please their readership or audience. *When* was it written? If it was produced a long time after the event in question it may not tell the full story. By answering these questions you will be able to form an opinion as to how valuable the source is as historical evidence. Don't fall into the trap of dismissing everything as un-reliable. There are problems with all sources of evidence but they are all we have got. Try to come to a *balanced judgement* as to relia-bility. In any case, sometimes sources which are very committed and subjective can tell us a lot about opinions at the time. The usefulness of a source depends very much on the question you are seeking to answer.

Each question in this book has a mark allocation indicated in brackets. The purpose of this is to give you some guidance as to how long your answer should be. Broadly speaking, you should spend twice as much time and space on a 4 mark question as on a 2 mark question.

1. Circles of poverty

Read the extract from William Booth on page 6:

a) Explain why Booth describes parts of England as 'this great lost land'. (Comprehension) (2 marks)

b) What does Booth mean when he writes that the borders of the 'great lost land are not sharply defined'? (Comprehension) (2 marks)

c) Do the language and tone of this extract suggest that Booth was sympa-thetic to the poor people he wrote about? (Source reliability) (5 marks)

2. Definitions of poverty

Read the extract from Adam Smith on page 2 and the extract from Charles Dickens on page 9.

a) Explain Smith's definition of poverty. (Comprehension) (2 marks)

b) To what extent does Dickens's character Mr Micawber share Smith's definition of poverty? (Comparison) (5 marks)

c) The extract on page 9 is taken from a novel. How far are novels useful as sources of evidence about social conditions? (Source reliability) (5 marks)

3. The experience of poverty

Read the extract by Jack London on pages 9-10 and the extract by Maud Pember Reeves on page 10.

a) In what ways could the family referred to in the extract on pages 9-10 be described as 'poor'? (Comprehension) (2 marks)

b) In what ways could the family referred to in the extract on page 10 be described as 'poor'? (Comprehension) (2 marks)

c) Both Jack London and Maud Pember Reeves were writing from a socialist perspective. How far does this invalidate their usefulness as sources of evidence about poverty in the early twentieth century? (Source reliability) (5 marks)

2 The Reform of the Poor Law

POINTS TO CONSIDER

This chapter is about the reform of the Poor Law in England and Wales in 1834, and especially about its significance. But to make judgements about its significance you need to understand a large amount of background - what was the Poor Law 'system' in the early nineteenth century; what was thought to be wrong with it, and by whom; and, what were the values and assumptions which underlay these criticisms? On your first rapid reading of the chapter try to clarify these background issues in your mind. Also pick out the technical terms used when studying the Poor Law and make sure you understand what they mean.

KEY DATES

1601 Establishment of the Poor Law

1782 Gilbert's Act. Parishes could combine to share the cost of the Poor Law in their area.

1789 Outbreak of the French Revolution.

1795 Magistrates in Speenhamland, Berkshire, agree to subsidise the wages of agricultural labourers from Poor Law funds.

1796 Publication of Thomas Malthus' *Essay on the Principle of Population*. Malthus calls for abolition of the Poor Law.

1798 Publication of Jeremy Bentham's *Pauper Management Improved*. Calls for a centralised Poor Law based on 'Houses of Industry'.

1817 Publication of David Ricardo's *Principles of Political Economy and Taxation*. Ricardo calls for abolition of the Poor Law.

1819 Sturges-Bourne Act. Allows the setting up of specialised committees ('Select Vestries') to supervise the Poor Law.

1824 Report of Select Committee on Labourers' Wages.

1832 Establishment of Royal Commission on the Poor Laws.

1834 Poor Law Amendment Act. Establishment of the New Poor Law.

From the end of the sixteenth century the English State had accepted some responsibility for the poorest and most vulnerable members of the population through a series of 'Poor Laws'. By the beginning of the nineteenth century the Poor Law was coming under increasing criticism from ratepayers, politicians and academic thinkers alike. In 1832 the government appointed a Commission to inquire into the workings of the Poor Law, and the report which the commissioners produced resulted in the 1834 Poor Law Amendment Act, a measure which fundamentally altered the way in which State and society treated the poor.

The 1834 Poor Law Amendment Act was one of the most

contentious pieces of nineteenth-century legislation, so it is not surprising that historians have engaged in a number of debates concerning its origins. The investigations of the Poor Law commissioners have come under particular scrutiny, with claims that their conclusions were prejudiced and based on incomplete evidence. Whether the report and the Act were motivated by a specific ideology or were just a pragmatic response to the problems of the time is another area of debate. Historians also disagree as to the significance of the Act itself. Some believe that it represented the victory of the newly enfranchised middle classes, whilst an alternative view is that the Act was an attempt to consolidate the traditional power of the rural landowning classes. Either way, there is no doubt that the New Poor Law and the workhouse system that went with it were hated by the poor themselves throughout the nineteenth and indeed into the twentieth century.

1 The Operation of the Old Poor Law

> **KEY ISSUE** What common assumptions were shared by the various 'systems' of poor relief which existed in England and Wales in the late eighteenth and early nineteenth centuries?

The Poor Law originated in the reign of Queen Elizabeth I. The Poor Law Act of 1601 established the main features of Poor Law for the next 233 years. The motivation for the Act was partly humanitarian, but mainly a concern for social stability, as it was widely believed among the property-owning classes that the presence of large numbers of unemployed poor was a potential threat to law and order. Under the Act the State took responsibility for those who were unable to support themselves. Each of the 15,000 parishes of England and Wales (the parish was the smallest unit of local government) was made responsible for orphans and those who were sick or elderly. Poorhouses could be built to accommodate these 'indigent' (unable to provide for themselves through no fault of their own) poor. The unemployed 'able-bodied' poor were to be provided with suitable work or, if none was available, support (cash or food). Support for the poor, or 'relief' as it was known, was financed through the rates, a local tax based on property values. Each parish appointed overseers who assessed the rates and determined who was in need of assistance. The overseers would sometimes distinguish the 'deserving' from the 'undeserving'. The parish vestry, a committee of ratepayers' representatives, was accountable to the local magistrates for the operation of the Poor Law.

These essential characteristics of the Poor Law remained unaltered until 1834, but there were some significant modifications. In the mid-seventeenth century, the Laws of Settlement were introduced. These laws were designed to protect an individual parish from being overwhelmed by the poor from elsewhere. They also aimed to strengthen authority and order by preventing the poor from moving around and becoming potential troublemakers in places where they were not known. The laws established that an individual's place of settlement was the parish in which he had been born, or the parish where he had lived for the previous three years. Overseers could order the removal of a person within 40 days of his arrival in a parish if it was considered likely that he might become an applicant for poor relief.

Gilbert's Act of 1782 was a second modification of the Poor Law. The Act was, in part, a response to the rising cost of the Poor Law. Under this Act individual parishes could group together to form larger Poor Law authorities. It was up to each parish to decide whether or not it wished to do this, but the advantage was that some costs could be reduced. For example, the parishes could share a common poorhouse rather than maintain one each. Gilbert's Act also gave legal support to the practice of giving relief to the able-bodied unemployed without forcing them to do some form of work for the parish if nothing suitable was available.

A third set of modifications to the Old Poor Laws came in the late-eighteenth century. In 1789 the outbreak of the French Revolution produced shockwaves which were keenly felt by the ruling classes across Europe. The subsequent wars between France and Britain contributed to a general economic downturn in the 1790s. Faced with increasing poverty and fearing that the same political upheaval might happen in England as was happening in France, magistrates in some parishes began to look for new ways to reduce the problems of the poor. In 1795, in the parish of Speenhamland, Berkshire, magistrates decided to subsidise low wages by paying agricultural labourers an allowance which increased according to the number of their children and the price of bread. This practice of subsidising the wages of those in work, rather than just supporting those without work, has subsequently become known as the 'Speenhamland system'. Historians now largely agree that this is a misleading name because it implies that what happened at Speenhamland was new and was the system adopted in all country areas. Wage support was not an entirely new feature of the Poor Law, and, although many magistrates in counties other than Berkshire now shared the same concerns about widespread distress, the approaches they adopted varied from the Speenhamland system in important ways. Whilst some parishes did pay allowances based on both bread prices and the number of children in a family, others paid just a flat rate allowance to each labourer. Some parishes took each child into consideration, while some paid only families with four or more children. Under the 'roundsman system', the Parish sent unemployed labourers round the local farms and paid an allowance to landowners who were prepared to take them on. Another variation was the 'labour rate' system. Here the Parish did not directly 'top-up' low pay, but landowners who took on unemployed labourers at a wage set by the parish were exempt from paying poor rates.

The Old Poor Law was not an early version of the welfare state with standard, nationwide levels of provision. Practice varied across the country and, in a large number of places, care for the sick and elderly was totally inadequate. In many parishes the level of support given to labourers was barely enough to ensure survival. But what all the eighteenth-century modifications to the Poor Law had in common was that they were genuine attempts to deal with the worst effects of poverty in their area. They reflected a tradition according to which the ruling groups in society accepted some responsibility for the welfare of the poorest. As such, the pre-1834 Poor Law was regarded by the poor themselves as an essential safety net in times of destitution and one from which they had a right to benefit. For example, the 1832 Commission of Enquiry into the operation of the Old Poor Law noted that in Yorkshire, 'relief is demanded as a matter of right, and sometimes with insolence'. It was this very notion of a 'right' to relief that came under increasing attack in the years before 1834.

2 The Attack on the Old Poor Law

> **KEY ISSUES** What did most late eighteenth-century writers think was wrong with the Poor Laws? What was most widely suggested as the solution to the problem of the Poor Laws?

The report of the Poor Law Commission of 1832 contained a range of serious criticisms of the Poor Law system and recommendations for its reform. But the Commission's report was certainly not the first publication to suggest an alternative method of dealing with the consequences of poverty. From the 1790s onwards some of the most prominent writers and commentators had put forward their own schemes for the relief of the poor. When the commissioners came to look at the Poor Law, there is no doubt that they were considerably influenced by these ideas.

a) Jeremy Bentham

Jeremy Bentham was a philosopher and writer whose most famous creation was the doctrine of 'utilitarianism'. This was the idea that all institutions should be tested to see whether they produced 'the greatest happiness for the greatest number' and should be reformed if they failed to pass this test of utility (usefulness). Utilitarian ideas were well known in the 1830s and are credited as key influences on the reforms of the Whig government in that decade. Crucially, Bentham's secretary in the later years of his life was Edwin Chadwick, the dominant force behind the 1832 enquiry into the Poor Laws and himself a committed 'Benthamite'.

Bentham's ideas on poverty and the Poor Law were outlined in his 1798 book *Pauper Management Improved*. His amazing proposal was to give entire responsibility for the poor to a body to be known as the National Charity Organisation. This was to be a profit-making, private company initially financed by a government subsidy. To begin with, 250 'industry houses' would be established to accommodate about half a million people. Bentham saw this rising to 500 houses, accommodating a million people - around 10 per cent of the total population. Poor relief would only be given to those who entered the house: support for people living in their own homes (known as outdoor relief) would be abolished. Life within an industry house would be deliberately hard, with strict supervision and discipline, long working hours and a meagre diet. Indeed, the conditions were designed to be less desirable than those outside the house so as to deter all but the most desperate from entering it. Those born in the workhouse would be kept there until their early twenties and would be encouraged to marry at an early age: Bentham wanted a young and disciplined permanent population within the house in order to maximise profits. He envisaged that he would be at the head of this centralised operation and had even invented a title for himself - Sub-Regulus of the Poor.

The National Charity Organisation embodied many features that were typical of the Benthamite approach - centralised administration, efficiency and universal minimum standards. Bentham was also keen to emphasise that the poor had a right to relief. However, his scheme was also typical in that it showed a complete disregard for the dignity, civil rights or emotional needs of the poor, and indeed treated them as a population of virtual slave prisoners. It also reduced all those who were poor to a state of complete dependence, something that distinguished it from the proposals of many other contemporaries.

b) Thomas Malthus and David Ricardo

Malthus and Ricardo differed in their analysis of the problem of poverty but they both shared the same radical solution - complete abolition of the Poor Laws. Thomas Malthus was a parson and economic writer most famous for his *Essay on Population* published in 1796. In this work, he developed his pessimistic theory that the expansion of population, so noticeable at the time, would inevitably outstrip the available food supply. 'Population', he wrote, 'increases in a geometrical, food in an arithmetical ratio'. Malthus predicted that while food supply might increase by, for example, 50 per cent, the population was likely to double in the same period. This meant that if the population continued to increase at its current rate, famine and disaster were sure to follow. Malthus went on to blame the Poor Laws for the population increase and for the state of the poor generally.

> 1 The labouring poor to use a common expression seem always to live from hand to mouth. Their present wants employ their whole attention, and they seldom think of the future. Even when they have an opportunity for saving they seldom exercise it, but all that is beyond
> 5 their present necessities goes, generally speaking, to the ale-house. The Poor Laws of England may therefore be said to diminish both the power and the will to save among the common people, and thus to weaken one of the strongest incentives to sobriety and industry, and consequently to happiness.

Abolishing the Poor Laws would, in the view of Malthus, lead to higher wages because, relieved of the burden of high poor rates, landowners would be able to afford to pay more. Abolition would also lead to smaller families because the incentive to have more children in order to get more relief would be removed. Malthus thought that all this would lead to greater prosperity. In later editions of his *Essay on Population* Malthus did concede the need for some family allowances and relief works for the unemployed, but it was his earlier thoughts which continued to influence policy-makers in the first half of the nineteenth century.

David Ricardo's economic ideas were influenced both by Malthus and the Scottish economist Adam Smith. In his 1817 *Principles of Political Economy and Taxation*, Ricardo combined Smith's belief in the free market, unfettered by any government controls or regulations, and the Malthusian fears about population. His 'iron law of wages' stated that any attempt to raise the pay of labourers through parish doles must necessarily impoverish the population because it would simply encourage dependency, idleness and fecklessness. He wrote that,

> 1 The nature of the evil points out the remedy. By gradually contracting the sphere of the Poor Laws; by impressing on the poor the value of independence, by teaching them that they must look not to systematic or casual charity but to their own exertions for support, that prudence
> 5 and forethought are neither unnecessary nor unprofitable virtues, we shall by degrees approach a sounder and more healthful state. No scheme for the amendment of the Poor Laws merits the least attention, which has not their abolition for its ultimate object.

c) Robert Owen and Thomas Paine

It would be wrong to think that all suggestions for Poor Law reform sought to reduce the role of the State in the alleviation of poverty. Rather than concentrating on the moral failings of the poor, the pioneer socialist Robert Owen blamed the economic system itself for creating poverty. Owen was a factory owner and had established a community in New Lanark, near Glasgow, based on his principles of co-operation. His solution to the problem of unemployment was for the government to settle labourers in new co-operative communities where they would be able to share the full benefits of their work without the exploitation of landowner or factory master. Owen's ideas were influential within the emerging working class but would have entailed a revolutionary overthrow of the existing social and economic order to be implemented. Not surprisingly, his solutions were rejected by property owners and policy-makers, both inside and outside parliament.

The radical writer Thomas Paine also had a much more sympathetic attitude to the poor. He criticised the Poor Laws for their inadequacy but urged that they be reformed so that they provided better support for the poor. In order to finance his reforms, Paine demanded the replacement of the poor rates by a land tax designed to hit the richer landowners. Paine also envisaged a redistribution of land and wealth from the rich to the poor. In the second part of his book *The Rights of Man*, published in 1792, he proposed an elementary social security system which would include family and education allowances for the support of children, and old age pensions. Thomas Paine was an important political thinker, and these were radical ideas. But Paine, like many other commentators of the time, also implied that the able-bodied unemployed would have to go to some form of workhouse if they wanted relief. Most of Paine's radical ideas were rejected by poor law reformers, but the workhouse concept was one which was not. Indeed, the idea that some sort of workhouse was the solution to the problems of poverty and poor relief became central to the investigation into the working of the Poor Laws.

3 The Commission of Inquiry into the Poor Laws

> **KEY ISSUE** Why was there widespread agreement among the propertied classes by 1832 that urgent action was required to reform the Poor Laws?

a) Why Did the Government Act?

In 1832 the Whig Government decided to set up a Royal Commission to inquire into the working of the Poor Laws. This decision was motivated by both long-term concerns and immediate problems. Concern at the way the Laws were operating had grown since the end of the Napoleonic Wars in 1815. Ratepayers had become increasingly agitated at the cost of poor relief, which continued to grow even in peacetime. During the Wars there was a general acceptance of the need to pay high rates to protect the poor in a time of crisis. Moreover, ratepaying farmers could afford higher rates due to the large profits they were making from high grain prices. After the Wars these ratepayers had expected poor rates to reduce and, as falling wheat prices eroded their profits, they began to demand this. In the immediate postwar period the total cost of poor relief rose from £5.7 million in 1815 to a peak of £7.9 million in 1817. After this, costs began to fall gradually so that expenditure in 1823 was back to £5.7 million. However, a series of poor harvests produced increasing agricultural distress in the 1820s, resulting in a rise in the cost of poor relief every year from 1823 onwards, reaching £7 million in 1831. Ratepayers began to fill the columns of local newspapers with letters complaining about this burden and demanding that something be done about it.

A second strand of criticism concerned the alleged corruption of local poor law administrators. Contracts for Poor Law work, for example supplying food, were routinely awarded to local tradespeople rather than put out to open tender. Concerned ratepayers suggested that this was just one way in which vested interests were exploiting the system. In 1817, a Select Committee of the House of Commons echoed these concerns, and the Committee's report was followed in 1819 by an Act of Parliament which allowed parishes to set up Select Vestries. These were small committees which could specialise in Poor Law administration and employ salaried assistant overseers to supervise it. By 1827, 2,868 parishes (almost 20 per cent of the total) had adopted the Act. However, in many cases the Select Vestries produced their own forms of corruption. For example, in 1832, 11 of the 20 members of the Morpeth Select Vestry had a vested interest in the sale of beer, and it was widely believed that generous relief payments ended up being spent in the local ale house or pub. By 1832, the number of Select Vestries had declined to 2,391, suggesting that they had failed to solve the problem. Ratepayers continued to press for more fundamental reform.

The third area of attack on the Poor Law concerned the effect that the so-called Speenhamland system was having on the attitudes and behaviour of the poor. Malthus had argued that the child allowances paid by some parishes encouraged labourers to have more and more children without considering the need to provide for them. The results of the 1821 census, which showed a significant increase in the population, were used to justify these fears. Commentators and ratepayers further claimed that the Speenhamland system was causing a 'demoralisation' of the workforce. Magistrates told the 1824 Select Committee on Labourers' Wages that under the 'Roundsman' system, labourers had no incentive to work hard or to respect their employers because they were convinced that the parish would look after their needs. The same committee also noted that another effect of Speenhamland was to reduce wages: farmers had no need to pay proper wage rates when they could get cheap, subsidised labour from the parish. Widespread agricultural disturbances in the early 1830s convinced the Government and the ruling elites that the rural population was getting out of control and that this was largely a result of the way the Poor Laws were operating. France was once again suffering political turmoil and the fear of revolution in Britain was real. The demand for reform became increasingly based on social and political concerns as well as economic motives.

b) How Did the Commission Conduct its Inquiry?

> **KEY ISSUE** How reliable was the information collected by the Royal Commission?

The Royal Commission on the Poor Laws consisted of seven members appointed in 1832 and a further two appointed in 1833. The two most influential commissioners were Nassau Senior, the Professor of Political Economy at Oxford University, and Edwin Chadwick, a lawyer who had been Jeremy Bentham's private secretary until the philosopher's death in 1832. Under the influence of Senior and Chadwick, the Commission set about the task of gathering a vast body of evidence concerning the operation of the Poor Laws. Twenty-six assistant commissioners were dispatched to carry out this investigation, armed with precise instructions from the commissioners on how to go about their work. They were to interview clergy, parish officers and magistrates, inspect parish documents, cross-examine witnesses, attend vestry meetings and follow up the replies to questionnaires which had been sent out by the commissioners.

There has been considerable criticism of the way in which the investigation was conducted. The historian Mark Blaug called the report 'wildly unstatistical', and there is considerable doubt about the accuracy of the picture it painted.[1] Of the 15,000 parishes in England and Wales, only 10 per cent were investigated. Even in those parishes which were visited, the questions asked were often confusing and therefore unlikely to elicit useful replies. For example,

> Have you any, and how many, able bodied labourers in the employment of individuals receiving allowance or regular relief from your parish on their own account or that of their families: and if on account of their families, at what number of children does it begin?

The overseers who filled in the questionnaire replies were often semi-literate and were certainly unaccustomed to dealing with such matters. Nevertheless, criticism of the Commission's methods needs to be tempered by a recognition that such a survey was in itself groundbreaking in an age with very primitive bureaucratic procedures. It would be unrealistic to expect modern standards of accuracy in a survey carried out in the early 1830s. However, what is fairly clear is that Chadwick and Senior had come to their conclusions even before the research was conducted and intended to use its findings merely as a tool to reform the Poor Laws in the fashion they had already chosen.

c) The 1834 Report

> **KEY ISSUE** What was the Report's most important recommendation?

The report of the Poor Law Commission was widely read. The 400 page 'extract' sold 15,000 copies before the full report, which was a massive document, was published. In the first part of the report, the Old Poor Law was attacked using examples from the research of the assistant commissioners. The second part of the report contained the Commission's conclusions and recommendations for reform. The central argument concerned the 'demoralisation' of the labouring class which, the commissioners claimed, had resulted from the Poor Laws:

1 It appears to the pauper that the Government has undertaken to repeal, in his favour, the ordinary laws of nature; to enact that the children shall not suffer for the misconduct of their parents, the wife for that of the husband, or the husband for that of the wife: that no
5 one shall lose the means of comfortable subsistence, whatever be his indolence, prodigality or vice: in short, that the penalty which, after all must be paid by some one for idleness and improvidence, is to fall, not on the guilty person or on his family, but on the proprietors of the lands and houses encumbered by his settlement. Can we wonder if the
10 uneducated are seduced into approving a system which aims its allurements at all the weakest parts of our nature - which offers marriage to the young, security to the anxious, ease to the lazy, and impunity to the profligate?

It was essential, it was claimed, to make greater distinction between the labourer who was poor, but independent, and the pauper:

1 Throughout the evidence it is shown, that in proportion as the condition of any pauper class is elevated above the condition of independent labourers, the condition of the independent class is depressed; their industry is impaired, their employment becomes
5 unsteady, and its remuneration in wages is diminished. Such persons, therefore, are under the strongest inducements to quit the less eligible class of labourers and enter the more eligible class of paupers ... Every penny bestowed, that tends to render the condition of the pauper more eligible than that of the independent labourer, is a bounty

10 on indolence and vice. We have found, that as the poor rates are at present administered, they operate as bounties of this description, to the amount of several millions annually.

The distinction between poverty, which the commissioners believed was a natural part of existence, and indigence (the inability to earn enough to live), which was not, was at the heart of the Commission's analysis. They believed that it was essential to separate the poor from the pauper, physically as well as psychologically. The Commissioners had been impressed by the operation in some areas, such as Southwell in Nottinghamshire, of deterrent workhouses - places where the able-bodied poor were forced to live and work if they wanted relief. The report recommended that all relief to able-bodied persons and their families, other than in such workhouses, should now be outlawed, and that, in order to enforce this workhouse system, a new central authority should be established with powers to compel parishes to co-operate.

4 The 1834 Poor Law Amendment Act

> **KEY ISSUE** What were the main terms of the Poor Law Amendment Act of 1834?

The Government responded to the Royal Commission report by drawing up a Bill which broadly reflected the recommendations in the report. Some of the powers of the proposed central authority were reduced during the debate, but the key recommendations of the report remained intact. The purpose of the 1834 Poor Law Amendment Act was to bring about radical reform of the system of poor relief in England and Wales. The Act contained four main mechanisms for achieving this: the establishment of a central authority to regulate the Poor Law, so that best practice could be enforced all over the country; the grouping together of parishes to form New Poor Law unions in order to benefit from economies of scale; the establishment of a workhouse in each union in which conditions would be worse than those endured by the most poorly paid independent worker, so that people would be deterred from entering them; and the proposal to reduce or abolish 'outdoor relief' for the able-bodied poor so that those seeking poor relief would have to go to a workhouse.

The central authority established by the Act was known as the Poor Law Commission, and was made up of three commissioners who were based in London and who were given wide-ranging powers to issue rules and regulations for the management of the Poor Law. Edwin Chadwick, whose ideas had inspired the 1834 Act, was made secretary to the Commission. He had hoped to be a commissioner in his own right and remained bitter that he had been given a subordinate role. The commissioners were initially supported by nine assistant commissioners whose job was to ensure that the decisions of the central authority were executed at a local level. However, their first task was to set up the New Poor Law unions. Under the Old Poor Law each of the 15,000 parishes in England and Wales was responsible for the relief of poverty in its own area. Now the aim was to amalgamate parishes into groups of about 30, each managed by a Board of Guardians. The Boards of Guardians were to be elected by the ratepayers of the whole area, with each parish having at least one representative on the board. Each union was to be responsible for the workhouse in its area. Under the Old Poor Law the local parish workhouse or poorhouse (where they existed - many parishes did not have one) had often been seen as a relatively unthreatening and even friendly institution. The workhouses of the New Poor Law were designed to project a very different image. In order to discourage applicants, conditions in the workhouses were supposed to be less appealing than those enjoyed by the poorest of labourers living outside the workhouse. This became known as 'the principle of less eligibility'. If applicants refused to accept workhouse life they were held to have 'failed the workhouse test'. The pre-1834 practice of providing relief to able-bodied paupers outside the workhouse was intended at first to be restricted and eventually to be abolished, so that those who failed the workhouse test would have no entitlement to poor relief.

5 The Significance of the Act

> **KEY ISSUE** What are the relative strengths of the three main interpretations of the Poor Law Amendment Act put forward by historians?

Historians have interpreted the 1834 Act in a number of ways. One interpretation is that the Act was a piece of naked class legislation, inspired by the middle classes, who had been enfranchised by the 1832 Parliamentary Reform Act and whose views had therefore to be taken seriously by most MPs. According to this view, Poor Law reform was a simple device to reduce the rate burden on property owners and force the poor to work for lower wages: the alternative was the harsh workhouse. The New Poor Law was part of a process by which the middle-class philosophy of individualism and the sovereignty of market forces replaced the older, paternalistic ideas that the rich had some responsibility for the poor. A variation on this theme has been put forward in Mitchell Dean's book *The Constitution of Poverty*.[2] Dean argues that 'the event of pauperism' (his term for the whole process of the New Poor Law) was crucial in establishing a capitalist market system in Britain where the working classes were forced to take responsibility for their own economic situation. Workers had to take employment at any wage rate and find alternative ways of coping with poverty because the State had withdrawn its traditional support. The 1834 Act withdrew the support traditionally provided by the State to those in need. From then on, according to Dean, workers were forced to accept the principles of the free market capitalist economy as the only alternative was the workhouse. This meant accepting lower wages and making some provision for their own protection, for example, through insurance schemes or friendly societies.

An alternative interpretation has been suggested by historians such as Anthony Brundage.[3] He claimed that the Act was in fact a way of maintaining the traditional social and economic powers of the landed elite. Faced with an increasingly turbulent and disaffected rural peasantry (as demonstrated by widespread rioting and disorder in the early 1830s), landowners decided to restore order and authority by enforcing a new system. Brundage argues that the Royal Commission had, after all, been appointed by the aristocratic, unreformed House of Commons. Moreover, his view is supported by the evidence that large landowners continued to dominate the administration of the Poor Law through the newly established Boards of Guardians.

Some historians have attempted to synthesise the two views by asserting that the New Poor Law served both to strengthen the power of the landowning elite and to introduce the capitalist market mechanism. According to M.J. Daunton, 'a new ideology had gained hegemony, without displacing the landed aristocracy from control of the central state'.[4] By this, Daunton implies that, although the landed aristocracy continued to dominate politics and control institutions like the Poor Law, they did so in the interests of the new capitalist classes. This attempt to reconcile the conflicting views on the significance of the 1834 Act has much to commend it, as it seems that the interests of both landowners and capitalists were strengthened by the legislation.

Whatever interpretation they put forward, most historians are in agreement on two things. Firstly, the 1834 Act was the most significant development in the history of poverty and welfare in the nineteenth century. The Act set the agenda for the debate on poverty for the next century and determined the nature of proposed alternatives. Secondly, the New Poor Law system was hated by the poor who had to live with the threat of the workhouse hanging over them. During the debate on the Act the MP William Cobbett claimed that the object of the Bill was 'to rob the poor man and enrich the landowner'. This certainly reflected widespread opinion amongst the poor. However, the new order not accepted without a fight. The 1834 Act had been passed by Parliament with little opposition. The Poor Law Commission's implementation of the new act throughout the country was to prove far more difficult.

Summary Diagram
The Reform of the Poor Law

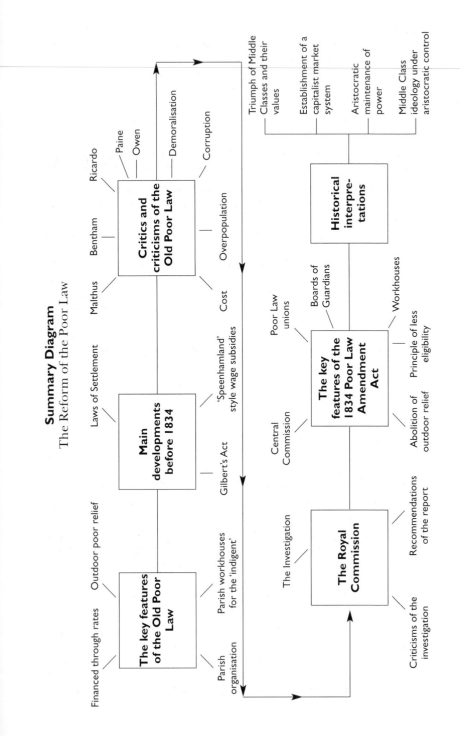

References:
1 Mark Blaug, *The myth of the Old Poor Law and the making of the New* (Jnl. of Economic History, 1963).
2 Mitchell Dean, *The Constitution of Poverty* (Routledge, 1991).
3 Anthony Brundage, *The Making of the New Poor Law 1832-39* (Hutchinson, 1978).
4 M.J. Daunton, *Progress and Poverty, An Economic and Social History of Britain 1750-1850* (OUP, 1995).

Working on Chapter 2

This chapter breaks down into five key elements. In order to prepare for questions concerning the causes of the 1834 Poor Law Amendment Act you need to know the essential features of the pre-1834 Poor Law. Once you have established these in your notes, you will then need to produce a list of the principle criticisms that were made of the old system. The third element is the work of the Royal Commission. You need to understand what the Commission recommended, but also the criticisms of the way it conducted its work. This is good material for looking at bias in historical sources and also the way language is used to make a point. It is crucial to have a clear grasp of the main features of the Act itself. Section 4 of the chapter will provide this information. Finally, you will need to distinguish the main historical interpretations of the Act.

Answering structured and essay questions on Chapter 2

History essay questions come in a wide variety of forms, but they tend to fall into two general categories:

- **Knowledge and understanding based questions.** These are designed principally to test your ability to recall (if the question is part of an exam), select and deploy historical knowledge accurately. They also test your ability to communicate your knowledge in a clear and effective manner.

- **Historical explanation and evaluation questions.** These are designed to test your ability to present historical explanations using appropriate knowledge and concepts, and your ability to arrive at a judgement based on your analysis. Such questions also require you to communicate your knowledge in a clear and effective manner.

In some exams, you may find yourself confronted with a one-part question, usually an explanation and evaluation type question. In other exams, you may find yourself facing a two-part structured question. This is likely to consist of a knowledge and understanding based question followed by an explanation and evaluation type question.

This Chapter is about the 1834 Poor Law Amendment Act and its origins. A typical two part structured essay question might be:

a) What were the main features of the 1834 Poor Law Amendment Act?
b) Why did the Government pass the 1834 Poor Law Amendment Act?

Part (a) of this structured question is a test of your knowledge and understanding. In order to answer it well you need to demonstrate a thorough knowledge and understanding of the 1834 Act. This requires you to outline the four main features of the Poor Law Amendment Act: the establishment of the Commission; the grouping together of parishes into Unions; the setting-up of deterrent work-houses based on the principle of less eligibility, and the proposal to abolish outdoor relief. A good answer will be accurate, will stick to the point and will deal with these features in a comprehensive fashion.

Part (b) of this structured question is an explanation and evaluation type question. The key historical concept involved is the concept of causation. To answer any question focused on causation you will need to outline the causes of the particular historical phenomenon or event, analyse the part each cause played in the overall explanation, and come to a conclusion as to the relative importance of the various causes that you have described.

Historians are always interested in the reasons why things happen. Firstly, they want to know the range of factors involved in causing an event or occurrence. Secondly, they want to analyse these factors. Were there long-term causes? These are the conditions which make a development possible, but they do not necessarily determine that it *will* happen. Short-term, or contingent factors are necessary to trigger the potential for an event into an actual event. In the case of the Poor Law Amendment Act, the long-term factors include the criticisms of the Old Poor Laws which had built up, particularly since the end of the eighteenth century, from writers like Malthus and Bentham. They also include the rising cost of the Poor Law, which had resulted in growing demands for reform. These factors meant that reform of the Poor Laws was probable, but other developments were necessary to turn this probability into actuality. The short term factors which did this include the concerns about demoralisation and disorder in the agricultural districts in the early 1830s, and the report of the Poor Law Commission. Make sure that you show the links between the different factors you describe. Conclude by indicating which factor or group of factors you believe to be most important.

You should check the mark schemes of your own examining board, but more marks may be allocated to part (b) of the question. You must divide the time and space you spend on each part in proportion to the marks available.

1. Critics of the old system

Read the extracts from Thomas Malthus and David Ricardo, both on page 20.

a) In the extract on page 20, what criticisms of the Poor Laws are made by Malthus? (2 marks)

b) To what extent does Ricardo agree with the views of Malthus? (4 marks)

c) How justified were the attitudes to the poor expressed in these extracts? (4 marks)

2. The investigation by the Royal Commission

Read the extract on page 23.

a) Explain the problem with the question in the extract. (2 marks)

b) What were the other flaws in the procedures of the Commission? (4 marks)

c) To what extent should the commissioners be criticised for the shortcomings of the inquiry? (6 marks)

3. The conclusions of the Commission

Read the extracts on pages 24-25.

a) What did the commissioners see as the main problem with the Old Poor Law? (2 marks)

b) Why might the views of the Commission have been particularly appealing to a middle-class audience? (4 marks)

c) How does the language and tone of the extracts suggest that the commissioners were influenced by moral judgements? (6 marks)

3 The New Poor Law in Operation

POINTS TO CONSIDER

This chapter is about the way the New Poor Law developed in the period 1834-1900. So it is about the process of change. You need to understand what the Poor Law Commissioners were trying to do and the obstacles that faced them. Examine the extent to which they achieved their objectives. How much change did they make happen? The third section of the chapter focuses on what life was like in the workhouse. You need to develop a sense of why the workhouses became such hated institutions. Finally, try to identify the key ways in which the Poor Law changed in the second half of the nineteenth century.

KEY DATES

1782 Gilbert's Act. Parishes allowed to join together to share the costs of the Poor Law in their area.

1834 Poor Law Amendment Act. Recommended the setting up of a central commission, the combination of parishes into unions and the establishment of the workhouse system.

1845 Andover scandal. Parliamentary inquiry in the following year reveals mistreatment of paupers at the Andover workhouse.

1847 Abolition of the Commission. Replaced by Poor Law Board under parliamentary control.

1852 Outdoor Relief Regulation Order. Acceptance that it is not possible to completely stop outdoor relief for the able-bodied.

1865 Union Chargeability Act. Made poor rates more equal between rich and poor areas.

1871 Local Government Board replaced Poor Law Board as the central Poor Law authority.

1886 Chamberlain circular. Government encourages local authorities to provide work schemes for the unemployed outside the Poor Law.

It is easy to think that the passing of an Act of Parliament automatically leads to its enforcement. This is not always the case. England in the 1830s was still a predominantly rural society where local identity was often stronger than the idea of the Nation. The centralisation implicit in the Poor Law Amendment Act was so ambitious that it was almost bound to provoke fierce resistance. This led to compromises in the implementation of the Law. Nevertheless the new system slowly became established as the most important institution for the relief of poverty in Victorian England despite the hatred which it inspired among its enemies.

1 The Implementation of the New Poor Law, 1834-70

> **KEY ISSUE** What obstacles faced the Commissioners in their attempt to set up the New Poor Law? How successful were they in establishing the new system?

The passing of the Poor Law Amendment Act in 1834 did not lead to the immediate establishment of a new system. On the contrary, the process by which Poor Law unions and workhouses were established was slow and varied considerably across the country. Despite their powerful constitutional position - they were not directly accountable to Parliament and they held both legislative and executive powers - the commissioners, to a great extent, had to rely on persuasion to enforce their will because there was no effective mechanism by which to make recalcitrant localities do what they were told. This meant that the assistant commissioners faced a number of problems when they attempted to implement the Act: they had to overcome local objections to their plans; they had to deal with surviving Old Poor Law administrations that were outside the new Law; and they had to persuade the new authorities to build new workhouses. When these initial tasks had been achieved, they still had to impose their will regarding the operation of the new system.

The first job of the assistant commissioners was to set up the new unions of parishes. To achieve this consultation with the local community was required and public meetings were called for this purpose. The original model for the organisation of the New Poor Law had proposed unions of equal size based on a market town and serving local parishes with a combined population of about 10,000, which meant on average getting the agreement of 30 parishes per union. This was a troublesome task: the local interest groups represented at the public meetings frequently refused to be slotted into such a neat pattern. Sometimes they were simply content with the way things were; sometimes they were afraid that contracts might be lost or costs might rise in the new unions. The assistant commissioners were under additional pressure to get quick results because the unions were also intended to be the administrative units for the registration of births, deaths and marriages which was due to commence in 1837. For both these reasons, compromises regarding the geography of the new unions were inevitable, and the shape of many reflected the interests of local landowners rather than the principles of the Act. Secondly, the Commission also had to contend with the 'Gilbert Unions'. These were areas which had already amalgamated their parishes for poor relief purposes under an Act of 1782 and which often refused to be brought into the new system. The same was true for those parishes which had established local poor relief committees known as Select Vestries under the Sturges Bourne Act of 1819. Both the Gilbert Unions and the Select Vestries remained outside the control of the Commission and the assistant commissioners were forced to work around these areas when planning the new unions.

Even after they had established a new union, the Commission faced a third difficulty. Although the commissioners could demand the alteration of an existing workhouse, they had no power to order the building of a new one. This could only be undertaken if a majority of members of the local Board of Guardians voted for it. As a result, it was possible for Poor Law unions to delay implementation of the new workhouse system. The majority of assistant commissioners showed an immense amount of political skill in persuading many Boards of Guardians to erect new workhouses, but where they were less persuasive the building of the new workhouse was considerably delayed.

The Commission's greatest and longest lasting problem was the difficulty of enforcing its will even after the administrative and physical structure had been built. At first sight, the setting up of the New Poor Law appeared to be a bureaucratic revolution with the establishment of a powerful central department with a team of inspectors dispatched to monitor local performance. But the reality was less dramatic. In 1836 the number of assistant commissioners was increased from 9 to 21, but even with this expansion it was hard for them to make a sustained impact. With responsibility for large areas, close supervision was very difficult. In 1834 one of the assistant commissioners, Colonel A'Court, complained that he had 'worked like a slave' to complete his inspection of Hampshire. He had been 'really shocked to reflect on the length of time it requires to inspect even one very insignificant district'. Six months later he added that he 'never had such hard work in my life. One more such district and I really think it would quite kill me'. In 1844 assistant commissioner William Day revealed that in a period of 20 weeks he had 'travelled a distance of 2596 miles, two-thirds of it with my own horses'. It became impossible to comply with the requirement that assistant commissioners visit each union in their area twice a year. This situation never improved and even by 1900 there was often only an annual visit.

The difficulties faced by assistant commissioners in the regions were mirrored by the Commission itself at the centre. Although they accumulated an impressive archive of reports and statistical returns and generated a mountain of instructions, it was impossible for the underpaid and understaffed Somerset House office clerks to cope efficiently with the deluge of information in which they found themselves drowning. The Commission's desire to play down failures and publicise success meant that administrative problems tended to be ignored rather than dealt with. Thus the Poor Law Commission exercised a much lower degree of effective centralisation than had been expected.

Yet, despite the problems they faced, the assistant commissioners were generally successful in establishing the new unions. By 1840, 14,000 English parishes with a total population of 12 million had been incorporated into Poor Law unions. Only 800 parishes, containing 2 million people, remained outside the system. The rural South of England was held up by the Commission as an early and over-whelming success. Most of the 350 new workhouses which had been built by 1839 were in this region. However, in Cornwall local resis-tance resulted in few new buildings and in those parts of the North where resistance was strongest the implementation of the Poor Law Amendment Act was much delayed. Very few workhouses were built in the West Riding of Yorkshire or in Lancashire until the 1850s and 1860s. In Todmorden the guardians went as far as to demolish their old workhouse and a replacement was not built until 1877.

The authors of the 1834 Act intended that all outdoor relief to the able-bodied would cease relatively rapidly. Building a new workhouse was intended to pave the way for this to happen. But in this key area of policy the Commission could only achieve their aims to a limited extent. In the South, the Commission began issuing orders prohibit-ing outdoor relief to the able-bodied poor from the late 1830s and the rural North came under similar regulations in 1842. In 1844 the Commission felt able to apply a general Outdoor Relief Prohibitory Order to all these unions with the result that probably three-quarters of the country was banned from giving outdoor relief. However, even in these areas, the rules could be interpreted in a flexible way, partic-ularly as the Order allowed the guardians to make exceptions in the case of accident or emergency. Assistant commissioner William Day complained to the Commission about the problem of enforcing the order to end outdoor relief to the able-bodied:

1 The people refused to acquiesce, and though compelled to submit to the law, took every advantage of evading it. Hence though the law was carried out to the *letter*, it has been paralysed as to the *spirit*, and the abuse of medical certificates has rendered the order a nullity. This is an
5 abuse I have reported over and over again to yourselves - but you have been unable to suggest a remedy.

Day's frustration reveals how difficult it was for the central authority to impose its will. Elsewhere, particularly in the new industrial towns, guardians continued to give outdoor relief to the able-bodied. The periodic trade depressions characteristic of the new industrial economy plunged thousands of workers at a time into unemploy-ment. There seemed little humane alternative but to continue outdoor relief, as even newly built workhouses could not cope with such numbers. The Commission made some attempt to bring these unions into line by issuing them with Labour Test Orders in 1842. These Orders stated that if outdoor relief were to be given, it could only be in return for some form of parish work such as stone breaking. The Commission also laid down that such relief should be paid at least partly in the form of food or fuel rather than totally in cash. But many unions continued to ignore the Orders and when the central authority tried to impose these instructions in 1852 there was an outcry. Guardians in the industrial North and in London realised that the stricter regulations would be difficult to enforce given the scale of poverty in their areas and forced the Commission to retreat. The 1852 Outdoor Relief Regulation Order withdrew both the compulsory labour rule and the instructions to pay some relief in kind. Following this the majority of unions were allowed to replace the workhouse by outdoor labour as the condition of relief. By 1871 only one in six unions was operating under the 1844 Order which banned outdoor relief to the able-bodied. One of the central policies of the New Poor Law had proved impossible to implement.

Certainly in the first three decades after it was introduced, the Poor Law Amendment Act was implemented in different ways and at different times in different parts of the country. The extent to which the Commission was able to enforce its will depended on a number of factors: the degree of local resistance by those who might come under the Act, the particular interests of those who held power in the region, the specific circumstances of the locality, and the degree of skill shown by the assistant commissioners in persuading the guardians to follow the central Commission's policies. However, despite all these obstacles, by the late 1860s, the overwhelming majority of parishes had been incorporated into poor law unions. Even though most paupers continued to receive outdoor relief, across the nation workhouses had sprung up as symbols of the new system and they housed over 150,000 inmates by 1870.

2 The Opposition to the New Poor Law

> **KEY ISSUES** Why did people oppose the 1834 Act? How widespread was the opposition to the Act? Was the opposition effective?

a) The Reasons for Opposition

The poorest sections of English society had many reasons to oppose the New Poor Law. The new system threatened to remove their traditional right to a basic level of support from their parish when they fell on hard times. The building of the new workhouses, or 'Bastilles' as they quickly came to be called, symbolised a harsh new form of authority under which the poor were to be punished for their poverty. The proposal that relief would only be given to those who entered the prison-like workhouses suggested that poverty itself had become a crime. Within the workhouses the strict regime was deliberately designed to be repellent. The new buildings were usually situated at some distance from the applicant's home, which made them seem more impersonal and threatening than the familiar, local parish institutions. This distance also fuelled the rumours that spread about the New Poor Law. The worst rumours were based on the fear that the workhouses had been built as extermination centres for the poor. After all, the Poor Law Amendment Act had been partly inspired by the writings of the Reverend Thomas Malthus who believed that the Nation's problems were caused by overpopulation. Assistant commissioner W. J. Gilbert reported that in Devon in 1836,

1   There was not anything too horrible or absurd to be circulated, and nothing too incredible for their belief. ... Amongst other ridiculous statements circulated, the peasantry fully believed that all the bread was poisoned, and that the only cause for giving it instead of money was the
5   facility it afforded of destroying the paupers; that all the children beyond three in a family were to be killed ...

The most extreme example of such anti-Poor Law propaganda was 'The Book of Murder!'. This was based on two anonymous pamphlets which discussed the possibility of gassing pauper children to reduce the population. Though the origins of these works are still unclear, it was easy for the terrified poor of the 1830s to believe claims that they had in fact been produced by the Poor Law commissioners themselves.

Under the old system, parish officials had made a distinction between the deserving poor, who were in trouble through no fault of their own, and those whose poverty was self-inflicted. Hard-working people were worried that they would now be thrown together with the roughest elements of society in the new workhouses. Bradford's radical anti-Poor Law leader Peter Bussey asked,

1   Did the new law draw a line of demarcation between the good and the evil? No. In the Bastille they found the most virtuous people crowded with the most vicious people on earth, and the treatment of one the same as the treatment of the other, and both worse than the common
5   felon.

Anti-Poor Law campaigners also claimed that the purpose of the workhouse was to drive down wages by forcing labourers to take any alternative form of employment, no matter how badly paid. When the Commission proposed a plan to move unemployed agricultural labourers north to the factory towns between 1835 and 1837, this seemed to confirm these claims. Mill owners had asked for the scheme specifically to limit rising wage rates in the North of England.

Many of those who had exercised authority under the Old Poor Law opposed the new system in order to protect their existing powers. In particular, those vestrymen or guardians who believed that they were already running a good system resisted change. As

Joseph Ellison, a member of the Dewsbury Board of Guardians, told the 1837 Parliamentary Select Committee on the Poor Law Amendment Act,

1   ... under no system of management could things be carried on more satisfactorily, both to the rate payers and to the paupers; and this is the opinion of nineteen-twentieths of that township where I reside. The general feeling is this, "What a pity that a system that has worked so
5   well, and has produced so much good, should now be broken up!" That is the universal exclamation ...

Ellison, and men like him, feared that the cost of building the new workhouses and maintaining the poor inside them would be excessive. Local authorities in urban areas were concerned that the new workhouses would be too small to deal with the flood of paupers expected in times of depression. On the other hand, it was argued that workhouses would stand empty and be a waste of resources in more prosperous times when work was plentiful. Rural ratepayers in many areas realised that outdoor relief cost only half the amount of indoor relief. Others feared that the abolition of traditional forms of poor relief would snap some of the paternalist bonds between rich and poor which operated as a form of social control. The evangelical reformer, Richard Oastler, said the new Law, 'lays the axe to the root of the social compact; it must break up society and make England a wilderness'.

One of the strongest arguments against the New Poor Law came from those who attacked the centralisation implicit in the new regime. The three commissioners were depicted as London-based tyrants seeking to impose their will on the entire Kingdom. One of the most powerful opponents of centralisation was the proprietor of *The Times* newspaper, John Walter. Walter was a Berkshire magistrate whose generous operation of outdoor relief under the old system had been singled out for criticism by the Royal Commission. During the debates on the Poor Law Amendment Bill in 1834, his newspaper had denounced the proposed new Law, claiming that it was,

1   ... against the deep-rooted and long formed habits of this nation, the principle of all which is that the people should be made to govern themselves as much as possible, at least in their domestic concerns and relations ... should it be carried, it will disgrace the statute-book which
5   contains Magna Charta and the Bill of Rights ...

The Commission's powers were indeed considerable and influential landowners were shocked at the degree of authority which the new body was given to intervene in the affairs of their locality. To them, the independence of the local parish and county was a cornerstone of English liberty and they never came to terms with the bureaucratic centralisation of the 1834 Act.

b) The Extent of the Opposition

In the rural South of England, resistance to the Act often took the form of riot and disorder as a means of defending the status quo. The case of the Amersham Union in Buckinghamshire is often quoted as a typical example of rural opposition. In May 1835, a mob took to the streets to prevent a small group of paupers being moved from Chesham to the new workhouse in Amersham. The local inhabitants seem to have seen this move as the beginning of the end for their old, familiar local workhouse and its replacement by a grim and distant 'bastille'. Despite, at first, preventing the transfer of the paupers, the demonstrators were eventually forced to give way after the local magistrates read the Riot Act, swore in special constables and called up reinforcements of both metropolitan police and armed yeomanry. Similar incidents occurred across the South of the country. Disturbances were reported in Kent in the Spring of 1835 and in East Anglia as late as 1844. However, on no occasion did these protests succeed in halting the implementation of the new Law.

In the industrial heartlands of the North of England resistance was more fierce. The campaign for extended legislation to protect factory workers known as the Ten Hour Movement - so called because its aim was to see legislation passed imposing a maximum 10 hour working day - was already well established and both leaders and supporters quickly mobilised to block what they saw as a new attack on working people. The hard edge of the northern anti-Poor Law agitation was felt in 1837 and 1838 when the Commission first attempted to introduce Poor Law unions into the industrial areas of Lancashire and the West Riding of Yorkshire. Chadwick had urged the commissioners to strike immediately in the North while there was relative prosperity but his advice was ignored. By 1837 the shadow of unemployment was starting to spread as a trade depression began and the threat of the workhouse was a real one for many workers. Huddersfield Guardian George Tinker wrote to the Commission in June 1837 to advise them of 'the perfect state of organisation into which the district has been put and the violent and unprincipled measures which are in operation to defeat your intentions'. He warned that 'in the present alarming state of the district it will be dangerous to put the Law into operation' and proceeded to describe a recent meeting of the local board:

1 ... the mob amounting to 6 or 8 thousand persons, led on by the notorious Oastler, broke open the gates of the workhouse and threatened to pull down the building if the Guardians did not immediately break up their meeting. It was with difficulty and by a very small majority that the
5 meeting was adjourned to another place in the town ... On the way to our second place of meeting, the guardians who were known to be favourable to the Law were repeatedly surrounded by the mob, and

their lives threatened if they attempted to carry it into effect. The magistrate present, R. Battye, Esq. placed us under the merciful protection of
10 Richard Oastler, and refused to read the Riot Act, notwithstanding that the heads of several of the constables had been broken and the windows of the room demolished with stones thrown by the mob. The opposition guardians during the meeting, regularly communicated its proceedings to the mob outside by haranguing them out at the windows
15 and by writing. Only eleven out of thirty nine guardians present voted for electing a clerk, and those who had the manliness to do so were individualised and the mob was promised that they should be afterwards acquainted with their names.

Violent protests also occurred in nearby Bradford in October 1837 and in Dewsbury in 1838. The Bradford riot was only quelled with the aid of troops who opened fire, though there were no fatalities. The South Lancashire Anti-Poor Law Association had established 38 local committees by 1838 and the most determined resistance came in the town of Todmorden. The campaign there was led by the Radical MP and enlightened factory owner John Fielden, whose tactics included closing down his own factory in protest at the election of guardians and refusing to pay his poor rates. Fielden's workers rallied to his

'Attack on the workhouse at Stockport', from the *Illustrated London News*, 1842.

defence when the board attempted to enforce payment and they proceeded to attack the homes of the local guardians. Once more troops were required to restore order.

In contrast to the scenes in the factory towns of Lancashire and Yorkshire there were few major disturbances elsewhere. In the North East the New Poor Law was established with relative ease and in London the Metropolitan Anti-Poor Law Association formed by Earl Stanhope in February 1838 made little impact. In the Midlands, a major pottery strike in Stoke-on-Trent in 1836 and a recession in the Nottingham stocking trade in the same year pushed many into poverty. But despite this, the workers of the Midlands took little direct action to frustrate the commissioners. However, the absence of violent protest should not be interpreted as signifying the complete acceptance of the new Act. The new Boards of Guardians represented local interests and were determined to interpret the Law in the way that best suited their particular situation. Although the poor themselves were not represented on the boards, the guardians had to include the degree of local resistance in their calculations. The decision whether or not to build a workhouse, and the extent to which outdoor relief was to be curtailed, were both related to the amount of protest and the anticipated reaction in each area.

There has been some historical debate on the nature of the opposition to the New Poor Law. The most common view has been that much of the opposition was a spontaneous reaction by people who wanted to maintain their traditional rights but had no coherent organisation or strategy. The only Anti-Poor Law Movement, according to these historians, was that which grew up in the factory towns of Lancashire and the West Riding of Yorkshire. In contrast, some historians have detected a more coherent set of beliefs amongst anti-Poor Law campaigners throughout the country.[1] What is clear is that the movement was short lived. Firstly, it was based on too broad an alliance: evangelical Tories and working-class radicals had different interests and were bound to disagree eventually. Secondly, in the late 1830s many anti-Poor Law campaigners turned to Chartism as a means of reforming the Poor Law. The failure to mount any significant opposition within the existing parliament convinced them that only a parliament elected by working men would repeal the Act.

3 The Realities of Life Under the New Poor Law

KEY ISSUE What was life like in the new workhouses?

The principle of less eligibility was a key aspect of the New Poor Law. The notion that conditions in the workhouse had to be less attractive than the conditions which the poorest independent labourer would experience inevitably meant that the new system had to be harsh.

However, the commissioners were very keen to make clear that their intention was not to introduce a system of deliberate cruelty. In fact, they claimed that their centralised and regulated system actually protected paupers by outlawing the abuses which existed under the Old Poor Law. Some historians have agreed with this view and have explained many of the worst scandals as representing the continuation of the Old Poor Law despite the efforts of the Commission. Other historians view the workhouse system as an example of institutionalised cruelty. It is possible to form some judgement regarding this debate by looking at life under the New Poor Law both for those excluded from relief and for those who entered the workhouse.

The poor who remained outside the workhouse because of their fear and hatred of it certainly experienced hardship. In his book *The Workhouse* Norman Longmate describes how in the mid-winter of late 1836 209 men applied for relief at Cuckfield in Sussex. When faced with the choice of the workhouse or nothing only 11 accepted the offer of the workhouse, and three of these decided to leave after a few hours.[2] The commissioners held the view that such people were obviously not really in need because they managed to survive outside the workhouse. However, without the possibility of any outdoor relief, life must have been grim indeed for those who refused indoor relief. Statistics for the period after 1834 suggested a decline in pauperism, but in places like Cuckfield this did not necessarily mean a decline in poverty.

Inside the workhouse every aspect of life was governed by detailed regulations laid down by the commissioners. The regime was designed to be unpleasant. On entering the workhouse paupers were forced to give up their own clothing and put on an ill-fitting uniform. Guardians were allowed to add variety to the clothing but they rarely did. Men and women were strictly segregated within the institution and no concessions were made for married couples. This aspect of the workhouse system was particularly resented and seemed to contradict Victorian ideas about the importance of the family. Nevertheless, depriving paupers of normal marital relations was a deliberate aspect of the regime, designed to increase the deterrent effect. It also discouraged pauper families from staying in the workhouse too long - an aspect of the Old Poor Law that had been much criticised.

The workhouse routine was designed to be both monotonous and arduous. The timetable was modified later in the century, but the changes from the original version were slight. In summer months the day began at 5.00am. Breakfast was eaten between 6.00 and 7.00am and was followed by work from 7.00am to 12.00pm. Dinner was taken between 12.00 and 1.00pm and a second work period stretched from 1.00 until 6.00pm. The supper hour was 6.00 to 7.00pm and the inmates had to be in bed by 8.00pm. There were compulsory prayers at the beginning and end of each day. The winter day began at 7.00am but was otherwise similar to the summer timetable. Work was to be

Picking Oakum: a London workhouse in 1905

deliberately hard and unpleasant. Oakum picking was a common task for both men and women: a number of old ropes, often knotted and tarred, had to be untwisted and unravelled inch by inch so that the fibres could be reused. Women were also set tasks such as washing, cleaning and cooking. Stone pounding and stone breaking were common tasks for men. This was hard, tedious, back breaking work. The most infamous work given to both sexes in the 1830s and 1840s was bone crushing, although this was prohibited in the second half of the century. Crushed animal bones were used as agricultural fertiliser and could be sold to local farmers. The dust and fragments produced from bone crushing were a health hazard and it was said that visitors could locate the bonehouse by its vile smell, especially in hot weather.

Anti-Poor Law campaigners frequently suggested that the poor were being starved in the workhouse, but the amount of food recommended by the commissioners was in fact greater than the average consumed by independent labourers (although much less than that provided for prisoners). However, in order to uphold the principle of less eligibility the meals were made to be as dull and boring as possible. Food had to be eaten at set times in large dining rooms and talking was not allowed at mealtimes. Guardians could choose between six official 'dietaries' which specified exactly how much paupers were allowed for each meal. Dietary no.2 consisted almost entirely of bread and cheese for breakfast, dinner and supper. This was the menu every day of the week apart from Sunday, when meat and vegetables were available for dinner, and Tuesday and Friday, when the paupers were treated to suet pudding and vegetables. Other dietaries replaced cheese with gruel for breakfast. Water was the only drink allowed for adults. Elderly paupers were allowed a few extras such as tea, and the local medical officer could prescribe additional nourishment for the sick. The monotonous diet provided basic nutritional requirements but the quality was variable and the food was often poorly prepared. In the 1830s many Boards of Guardians increased the humiliation of the workhouse inmates by refusing to provide cutlery and paupers had to eat with their hands or drink gruel or soup from the bowl.

Discipline in the workhouse was strict, but once again the commissioners saw this as progressive. Under the Old Poor Law workhouse inmates had been subject to the arbitrary authority of overseers who were not constrained by any set of clear rules and who were often able to abuse their charges without fear of the consequences. Under the new Law an elaborate set of instructions specified exactly what workhouse masters could and could not do. Adults and girls could not be beaten and, although rations could be reduced, they could not fall below a certain minimum. Most workhouses had punishment cells and the regulations allowed paupers to be confined in them for a range of minor offences. Being in the wrong part of the building, failing to work hard enough, making too much noise or disobeying the authorities were all punishable acts. Paupers also needed permission to leave the workhouse or to be visited by friends or relatives. So, although the regulations were partly designed to control workhouse officers, they also represented a petty form of tyranny which dominated all aspects of an inmate's life.

Despite the Commission's rules, well publicised incidents of abuse occurred on a number of occasions. In March 1846, a Select Committee of the House of Commons was appointed to investigate allegations of wrongdoing at the Andover workhouse in Hampshire. This revealed an appalling state of affairs. The inmates had been systematically underfed: even the children's milk was watered down. The situation had first come to light when one of the guardians expressed concern over what was happening in the bonehouse and the enquiry confirmed that these concerns were justified. Paupers had been so undernourished that they had taken to eating the marrow and rotting meat on the bones they had been set to crush. Children had been so starved that they had eaten the raw potatoes thrown out for the workhouse pigs. The workhouse master, Mr. M'Dougal, was shown to be a drunk and a bully who inflicted cruel punishments on those under his rule. Beatings were inflicted on children and confinement in the cells followed the slightest infringement of the rules. Some inmates were forced to spend the night in the workhouse mortuary as a punishment. Burials were conducted as cheaply as possible, with infant corpses receiving the minimum of ceremony. Witnesses also reported numerous instances of sexual abuse of female inmates by both M'Dougal and his 17-year-old son. The report of the Select Committee found that the workhouse master and matron were unfit persons to hold such positions and also condemned both the Andover Board of Guardians and the Poor Law commissioners for allowing such a situation to go unchecked. Although M'Dougal was forced to resign, he received no further punishment. Nevertheless the revelations of the enquiry were widely reported, had a powerful effect on public opinion and were to lead to the demise of the Commission itself.

The evidence about workhouse life has led to a number of different interpretations of the New Poor Law in terms of its harshness. The Andover scandal was an extreme example of how the workhouse system could produce horrific results. But whilst the Andover case was unforgivable it was also untypical. Many of the other alleged atrocities produced by opponents of the New Poor Law have been shown to be either gross exaggerations or complete inventions. This has led some historians to state that the New Poor Law was no more cruel than the Old Poor Law and to agree with the commissioners' claims that their centralised control did indeed reduce the opportunities for brutal workhouse masters or penny-pinching guardians to misuse their power.[3] Other historians have remained critical. They point out that a system which was designed to be harsh inevitably encouraged some of those in authority to overstep the mark in their enthusiasm to deter the poor from applying for relief.[4]

A third interpretation emphasises the way in which the institutional arrangements of the workhouse system inflicted a form of psychological as opposed to physical cruelty.[5] Silent mealtimes, monotonous work and the absence of even the smallest of extra comforts were all matters of deliberate policy, not accident. The petty rules, strict discipline and prison-like uniforms all combined to deny the identity and dignity of the pauper and take away his or her individuality. Moreover, in the interests of deterrence the commissioners fostered the idea of the workhouse as a grim place from which the poor would do well to stay away. The commissioners were thus responsible for creating a climate of fear which pervaded working class life for over a century. Ironically, the propaganda of the anti-Poor Law campaigners helped to strengthen this image and terrify people into avoiding the workhouse. The cartoon on page 46, which appeared as a wall poster, is a good example of the way in which aspects of workhouse life could be exaggerated.

An anti-workhouse poster, circa 1840

4 The Development of the New Poor Law During the Nineteenth Century

> **KEY ISSUE** What were the major developments in the operation of the Poor Law in the period after 1834?

By the 1860s the New Poor Law was well established even though it was being implemented in different ways in different parts of the country. However, the setting up of the new administration and the building of new workhouses did not mean that the system stopped developing. Some aspects of the New Poor Law did remain consistent throughout its history, but many others changed in response to outside pressures and new ideas. These developments occurred in four main areas: central administration; finance; outdoor relief; and the provision of services for children, the sick and the elderly.

a) The Central Administration of the Poor Law

The three London based commissioners established by the 1834 Act had, in theory, a remarkable degree of authority. They could both make regulations and enforce them without reference to Parliament. This had been thought necessary in order to set up and enforce the New Poor Law as quickly and as efficiently as possible. It had been envisaged that the Commission's extraordinary powers would be of a temporary nature and the 1834 Act had limited its life to an initial period of five years. During this period, particularly in the late 1830s, the central administration was subjected to heavy criticism from the opponents of the Poor Law with *The Times* referring to them as 'The Three Bashaws of Somerset House'. (A 'Bashaw' was an authoritarian military governor in the Turkish empire and a popular symbol of tyrannical rule.) As a result of this pressure Parliament only renewed the Commission's powers on a year to year basis after 1839. By 1842 the direct resistance to the New Poor Law had passed its peak and Parliament was prepared to give the Commission another five years in office. However, they also reduced the effective power of the Commission by cutting back the number of assistant commissioners to nine, the establishment originally proposed in the 1834 Act.

In 1847 Parliament decided that it was time to replace the Somerset House administration. The main cause of the Commission's demise turned out to be the Andover scandal (see pages 44-45). The Select Committee's report had condemned the central authority as well as the local administration. In particular, the MPs had described as a 'cruel injustice' the commissioners' treatment of Henry Parker, the assistant commissioner responsible for Andover. Parker had been made the scapegoat for the wrongdoing at the workhouse and had been dismissed after his initial report on the affair. The dismissal of another assistant commissioner was also attacked as 'irregular and arbitrary'. The Select Committee's investigations had also revealed the tensions within Somerset House, especially the animosity between Edwin Chadwick and the commissioners. Chadwick had never reconciled himself to his subordinate position as secretary to the Commission and used the opportunity provided by the Andover enquiry to criticise his employers. The picture revealed by the Select Committee convinced Parliament that they needed to exert a tighter authority over the central administration of the Poor Law.

The Poor Law Commission was replaced in 1847 by a new body, the Poor Law Board. This body consisted of a President, two secretaries and a number of Cabinet Ministers who sat on the board *ex officio*. Although the Cabinet Ministers actually had little direct involvement in the administration of the Law, both the President and one of the two secretaries were usually MPs. The intention was to provide more direct political control over Poor Law administration so as to make it more responsive to public opinion.

By the 1870s, there had been a significant extension of government interest in the areas of health and welfare, partly due to the political pressures resulting from the extension of the franchise in 1867. As new social legislation was usually enforced through local authorities, it seemed logical to combine the responsibility for the Poor Law with responsibility for the rest of local government. Therefore, in 1871, the Poor Law Board was replaced by the Local Government Board. Because the Poor Law Board had been successful in avoiding new scandals like Andover, and because health and welfare issues now had a higher profile, the government retained direct control over the new authority. From 1871 onwards, the President of the Local Government Board was normally a cabinet minister.

b) Poor Law Finances

Until the 1860s each parish had to pay for its own paupers. This meant that some rich landowners with large estates paid very low poor rates because their parish had only a few paupers. On the other hand, the parishes with the largest numbers of paupers paid the largest amounts of money and, therefore, charged the highest rates despite the fact that they were often the poorest parishes in the union. In some areas, this system had resulted in financial crisis with heavily pauperised parishes unable to raise the necessary sums. The 1865 Union Chargeability Act attempted to remedy this problem. The cost of poor relief payments was transferred from the individual parish to the union as a whole. Each parish contributed to the common union fund on the basis of its rateable value, not on the number of paupers it had. This spread the burden over the entire union and meant that the poorer parishes were subsidised by the wealthier. Ratepayers were charged according to the value of their property and the reform meant that within each union the rich now paid more than poorer inhabitants. These changes resulted in a more equitable system of Poor Law finances.

Many Boards of Guardians had refused to upgrade the facilities in their workhouses to provide for children, the sick and the elderly because of the cost involved. Most boards were dominated by middle-class guardians who had pledged to keep the poor rates as low as possible. The 1869 Poor Law Loans Act helped to improve this situation. From 1863 guardians had been authorised to raise loans for building works from the Public Works Commissioners. The 1869 Act extended the repayment period on these loans from 20 to 30 years. This meant that the amount that had to be repaid each year was reduced and so, therefore, were the rates. This Act, along with the other financial changes of the 1860s, made it possible for guardians to consider higher expenditure on the Poor Law without raising the poor rates to unacceptable levels.

c) The Persistence of Outdoor Relief

The authors of the 1834 Act had aimed to abolish outdoor relief completely. The relaxation of the ban on outdoor relief in the 1850s was a response to the resistance campaigns against the implementation of the workhouse system. But, by the late 1860s, the results of this policy were becoming a cause for concern. The 1860s had witnessed an increase in spending on outdoor relief of over 25 per cent and the ratio of outdoor paupers to the total population had increased from 1 in 27 to 1 in 25. One significant contribution to this state of affairs had been the need to relieve the textile operatives who had been thrown out of work in the Lancashire 'cotton famine' caused by the American Civil War. Guardians in other areas continued to see outdoor relief as the cheap option: in the 1860s the cost of maintaining a pauper in the workhouse was around six shillings a week whereas outdoor relief was about two shillings. These small outdoor payments were given on the assumption that recipients would supplement them by earnings from low-paid work or charity, since it was clear that the payments alone were not enough to live on. When the Poor Law Board was replaced by the Local Government Board in 1871 the new body was quick to issue a circular attacking outdoor relief and restating the principles of the 1834 Act:

1   ... the increase in the cost of out-door relief is so great, as to excite apprehension; and to suggest that measures should be taken, not only to check any further increase, but to diminish the present amount ... It has been shown that in numerous instances the Guardians disregard the
5   advantages not only to the ratepayers but to the poor themselves from the offer of in-door in preference to outdoor relief. A certainty of

obtaining out-door relief in his own home whenever he may ask for it extinguishes in the mind of the labourer all motive for husbanding his resources, and induces him to rely exclusively upon the rates instead of
10 upon his own savings for such relief as he may require. It removes every incentive to self-reliance and prudent fore-thought on his part, and induces him, moreover, to apply for relief on occasions when the circumstances are not such as to render him absolutely in need of it.

The drive to reduce outdoor relief in the late nineteenth century was aided by the growing number of charity organisations which were being established in the period (see Chapter 4). Charity payments seemed to be targeted at the 'deserving' poor and allowed the Poor Law authorities to take a tougher line with paupers whom they could classify as indigent and 'undeserving'. Deterrent workhouses of an especially hard nature were opened in places such as Poplar in East London. Only able-bodied paupers were invited to the Poplar workhouse (separate arrangements were made for the sick and the elderly) and the work set there was much heavier than in other workhouses. The combination of a more aggressive insistence on workhouse relief and the benevolence of the charities brought the desired effect: the number receiving outdoor relief had reduced significantly by 1900. Although the workhouse population had risen by the turn of the century, the proportion of paupers in the total population had declined from 4.7 per cent in the 1860s to around 2.5 per cent in 1900.

A final development also helped to keep the level of pauperism down. Following a trade depression and the onset of mass unemployment in the 1880s, Joseph Chamberlain, President of the Local Government Board, issued a famous circular to Boards of Guardians in 1886. This recommended that they provide additional work

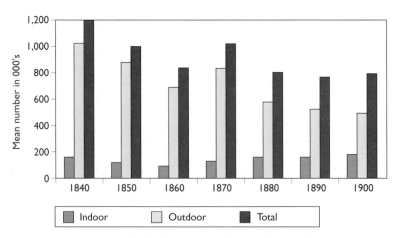

Poor relief in England and Wales 1840-1900

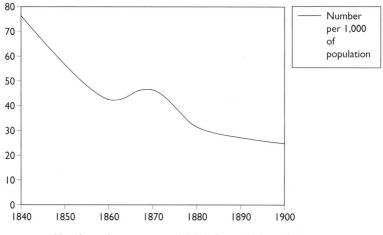

Number of paupers per 1,000 of population 1840-1900

schemes such as street cleaning and paving, to 'persons whom, owing to precarious condition and circumstances, it is undesirable to send to the workhouse, or to treat as subjects for pauper relief.' Though limited in its effect, this initiative clearly echoed some of the practices of the Old Poor Law and represented a further retreat from the principles of 1834.

d) The Development of Specialist Services for the Poor

Chadwick's original plans for the Poor Law had proposed separate institutions for different categories of pauper: the able-bodied, the elderly, the sick and children. Because of the costs involved, this plan was never carried out and, although there was segregation in the new workhouses, all the different categories of pauper were housed within the same institution. Even in the early days of the Commission this caused problems. Guardians did not want to separate children from their mothers, but neither did they want these children 'contaminated' by the rougher elements to be found in the female wards. The usual compromise was to allow infants under two to stay with their mothers but to remove children over two years old to separate quarters. The emphasis on maintaining the deterrent aspects of workhouse life had, in the first half century of the New Poor Law, frustrated attempts at improving facilities for children, the sick and the elderly. When the Local Government Board began its crackdown on outdoor relief in the 1870s it faced a problem. For, although the logic of the Poor Law supported a toughening of conditions for the able-bodied poor, it was hard to justify any imposition of such conditions on those who were poor through illness or age. By the late nineteenth century there was an increasing awareness that the elderly, children and those who were sick had to be treated in new ways.

In fact, elderly paupers had always been regarded in a somewhat different light to the 'able-bodied' by those who managed the Poor Law. The Royal Commission had hoped that 'the old might enjoy their indulgences' even though the 1834 Act itself made little direct reference to the elderly. Workhouse dietaries suggested that the elderly should get a little extra but this was not intended as a right. Dietary no. 2 recommended an ounce of tea and some milk and sugar for those over 60, but an additional meat pudding dinner on Thursdays was only given to those 'for whose age and infirmities it may be deemed requisite'. Similarly, dietary no. 3 only provided for the old to receive extra food 'if deemed expedient to make this change'. Deterrent workhouse conditions for the elderly were to an extent consistent with the general thinking behind the New Poor Law. Without some incentive to do otherwise, it was feared that the elderly would automatically throw themselves on the rates. Labouring people, according to this way of thinking, should put something aside for their old age or ensure that they had families to support them. If they failed to be prudent that was their own fault. Consequently, in the early years of the new system the elderly were given deterrent work and endured similar conditions to the younger workhouse inmates.

By the middle of the century the attitude towards elderly paupers was beginning to change. The compulsory separation of elderly couples was relaxed in 1847 when the Poor Law Board ruled that separate bedrooms had to be provided for couples over 60 if they were requested. However, little was done to implement this ruling and in 1895 only 200 married couples had their own workhouse rooms. Enquiries into the condition of the aged poor led the Local Government Board to issue specific advice on the treatment of the elderly in 1900. The Board recommended that adequate outdoor relief should be given to the 'aged deserving poor' and that where indoor relief was necessary old people should be 'granted certain privileges which could not be accorded to every inmate of the workhouse'. These privileges were to include extra day rooms, flexible eating and sleeping times, greater visiting rights, and the compulsory provision of tobacco, dry tea (so that they could make a cup whenever they wanted) and sugar. In these ways conditions for aged paupers in the early twentieth century were better than they had been in the mid-nineteenth. Nevertheless, despite these improvements, the possibility that they would end their days in the workhouse remained a dreadful worry for many old people.

Children under the age of 16 constituted approximately one-third of the pauper population throughout the nineteenth century. Workhouse schools had been established from the 1830s and were the earliest forms of state education. They aimed to give pauper children the opportunity to escape from the poverty of their parents though a sound basic education. However, there has been some debate about how effective these schools actually were.[6] Financial constraints frequently resulted in the employment of inadequate teachers, and the stigmatising of all paupers encouraged some guardians to neglect their schools. Nevertheless, Poor Law schools in some areas provided higher standards of basic education than comparable voluntary schools, although their curriculum was narrower. After 1846, a government grant was available to pay the salaries of Poor Law teachers. Some ambitious industrial schools had been built by urban unions in Leeds, Manchester, London and other cities in the middle decades of the century. These schools were separate from the workhouses, served the pauper children of a whole district, and concentrated on what Commissioner George Nicholls described as 'honest and useful industrial courses' which would equip pauper children to become 'good servants or good workmen'. The best of these institutions were heavily influenced by the ideas of Dr. James Kay (later Sir James Kay-Shuttleworth), an assistant commissioner who went on to become the First Secretary to the Privy Council's Committee on Education. However, they were increasingly seen in a negative light as the desirability of segregating pauper children began to be questioned. The creation of state run Board schools after the 1870 Education Act allowed most pauper children to be integrated into mainstream education.

Illness was one of the chief causes of poverty yet the authorities paid relatively little attention to it in the early phase of the New Poor Law. The 1834 Act had made only a brief mention of the possibility of providing medical relief. Medical officers were appointed by the Boards of Guardians in each union but it was the Workhouse masters and poor law relieving officers who decided whether or not a pauper was entitled to medical relief. The result of this arrangement was that medical relief was kept to a minimum as the authorities tried to keep costs down: in 1840 only £150,000 out of a total Poor Law expenditure of £4.5 million went on medical services. Basic infirmaries had been attached to workhouses under the Old Poor Law and this practice continued after 1834. However, the infirmaries were intended only for the short-term use of the workhouse inmates and most were unable to meet the demands of the long-term sick who needed care. Conditions were poor and the infirmaries were inadequately staffed. Medical officer Robert Tatham described the floors in the workhouse hospital in Huddersfield as,

> … filthy. I don't think they had been washed down throughout the hospital, from the time of its being opened; marks of uncleanliness presented themselves nearly everywhere; cobwebs hung from the ceilings; the coverings of the beds were very deficient - mere rags some of

5   them; some of the blankets would hardly hold together if you would
shake them ...

The conditions in Huddersfield had come to light following an
outbreak of typhus. The two nurses in the hospital were themselves
pauper inmates and one of them was frequently ill. This state of
affairs was typical of many workhouse infirmaries, and in the
first 30 years of the New Poor Law little was done to raise
standards.

Improvements in Poor Law medicine really date from the late
1860s when public opinion was alerted to these problems by an
enquiry conducted for the medical journal *The Lancet*. This had
revealed some scandalous conditions in London workhouse infirmaries and forced the Government to take action. Gathorne Hardy,
President of the Poor Law Board, signalled a major change in attitude when he blamed the failures of medical care on the deterrent
nature of the workhouse system. 'The sick', he declared, 'are not
proper objects for such a system'. The way to take the sick out of the
deterrent system was to establish hospitals which were separate from
the workhouses. In London, this was made possible by the 1867
Metropolitan Poor Act. This amalgamated the medical services of
the different London Poor Law unions and created the new
Metropolitan Asylums Board, which became the hospital authority
for the whole of the capital. As with the other financial reforms of the
1860s, spreading the cost of poor law expenses over a larger
area enabled improvements to be made. By 1882, six Fever hospitals,
four asylums and 20 infirmaries were in operation in London.
Across the country Poor Law authorities began to follow this lead
and between 1861 and 1891 1000 beds per annum were being added
to public provision. These were promising signs, although the quality
of medical care remained variable. By 1900, the Poor Law was
providing a national, state-funded system of basic medical care. Some
historians have seen in this process the origins of the National Health
Service and Poor Law buildings have continued to be used as the
basis of major hospitals into the late twentieth century.[7]

References

1   J. Knott, *Popular opposition to the 1834 Poor Law* (Croom Helm, 1986).
2   Norman Longmate, *The Workhouse* (Temple Smith, 1974), p. 78.
3   David Roberts, *How cruel was the Victorian Poor Law?* (Historical Jnl. VI,
    1963), pp. 97-107.
4   Longmate, *The Workhouse*.
5   Ursula Henriques, *How cruel was the Victorian Poor Law?* (Historical Jnl.
    XI, 1968), pp. 365-371; M A Crowther, *The Workhouse System*, (Methuen,
    1981), p. 270-271.
6   Frank Crompton, *Workhouse Children* (Sutton, 1997).
7   Crowther, *The Workhouse System*, p. 269.

Working on Chapter 3

This chapter deals with the setting up of the New Poor Law and its development up to 1900. You need to have a good grasp of the process by which the new system was set up in the 1830s and 1840s as well as the ways in which it changed and developed throughout the nineteenth century.

Answering structured and essay questions on Chapter 3

Questions on the implementation and operation of the New Poor Law often demand both an understanding of the main features of the system and an evaluation of two sides of an argument. Two areas of debate are particularly common. Firstly, there is the relationship between the aims of the 1834 Poor Law Amendment Act and the effect of the Act. A two part structured question on this topic might be:

a) What problems was the 1834 Poor Law Amendment Act meant to solve?
b) How effectively did the 1834 Poor Law Amendment Act solve these problems?

You need to identify the problems that the Act was meant to solve clearly (see also Chapter 2): the problem of rising costs; the 'demoralisation' of the labouring classes; social unrest; concern at the inconsistent application of the Poor Laws across the country. Remember that the authors of the Act aimed to deal with *pauperism*, not *poverty*. The authors of the Act wanted a tightly regulated system which had well run but deterrent workhouses and no outdoor relief. Part (b) of the question requires you to examine the evidence in order to decide the extent to which the New Poor Law did or did not achieve these objectives. You will need to come to a clear judgement in your conclusion: did the Act *mainly solve* the problems it was designed to tackle or did it *mainly fail* to do so? Did it succeed in some areas but not in others?

A second type of question concentrates on the operation of the new Law, e.g.

a) Why did so many people oppose the Poor Law Amendment Act of 1834 ?
b) How far would you agree that the Poor Law Amendment Act of 1834 was 'unworkable as well as unpopular'?

Part (a) is a test of knowledge and understanding. To answer part (a) you will need to outline the main arguments of the anti-Poor Law campaigners regarding the workhouses, the Commission, the attempted abolition of outdoor relief and the perceived attack on the living standards of the poor. Part (b) requires analysis as well as

Summary Diagram
The New Poor Law in Operation

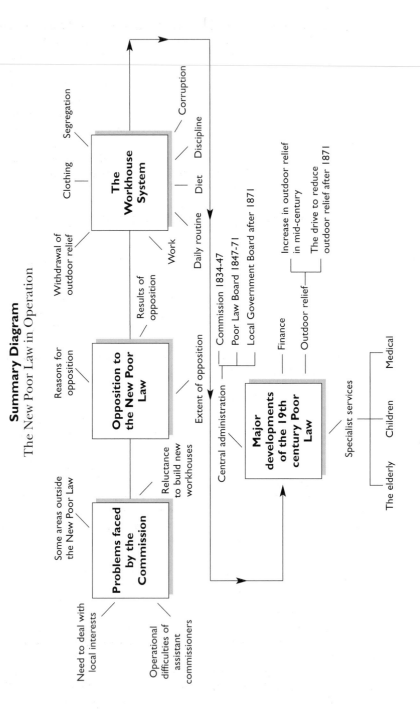

knowledge and understanding. To answer part (b) you will need to examine the evidence for and against the proposition that the Act was unworkable and for and against the proposition that it was unpopular. To determine the extent to which it was unworkable you will need to include the difficulties faced by the assistant commissioners, the variety of implementation across the country and the persistence of outdoor relief. The extent to which the Act was unpopular can be judged to some extent by the degree of opposition in the 1830s and 1840s but you must also comment on reactions to the Poor Law system throughout the century. It is important that you come to a clear judgement as to how far it was 'unworkable as well as unpopular' in your conclusion.

Source-based questions on Chapter 3

1. Arguments against the New Poor Law
Read the extracts on pages 37 and 38 (from Peter Bussey, Joseph Ellison and *The Times*)

a) What were the arguments put forward in *The Times* against the New Poor Law? (2 marks)

c) To what extent do the three extracts agree in their analysis of the New Poor Law? (6 marks)

b) In the light of their origins, what motives might have inspired each of the three authors? (6 marks)

2. The struggle to implement the Act
Read the accounts by William Day (page 35), W.J. Gilbert (page 37) and George Tinker (pages 39-40) and look at the cartoon on page 40.

a) How did the actions of 'the mob' obstruct the establishment of the New Poor Law in Huddersfield? (2 marks)

b) To what extent do the three accounts indicate similar problems for those setting up the New Poor Law? (6 marks)

c) How far do these extracts and the cartoon provide reliable accounts of the opposition to the New Poor Law? (6 marks)

3. Conditions within the workhouse
Look at the cartoon on page 46.

a) What message is the illustrator trying to convey about conditions in the workhouse? (2 marks)

b) In what ways does the illustrator exaggerate the harshness of work-house life? (4 marks)

c) What is the usefulness and what are the limitations of this cartoon to a historian studying the workhouse system in the nineteenth century? (6 marks)

4. Indoor and outdoor pauperism

Look at the statistical information on pages 50 and 51.

a) How did the number of outdoor paupers fluctuate in the period 1850 to 1900? (2 marks)

b) Explain the reasons for the fluctuations in outdoor pauperism 1850-1900. (4 marks)

c) Do the statistics on total pauperism and indoor pauperism confirm that the 1834 Act failed to achieve its aims? (4 marks)

d) Why did the number of indoor paupers rise so rapidly in the 1870s? (4 marks)

4 Charity and Self-Help

POINTS TO CONSIDER

This chapter looks at the alternatives to the Poor Law which were available to the Victorian poor. You will need to understand the idea of 'self-help' as this underpinned many of these alternatives. Examine each of the alternatives - charity, friendly societies, trade unions, co-operatives, informal neighbourhood groups. Concentrate on understanding how this type of welfare worked. What were the strengths and weaknesses of each?

KEY DATES

1843 Metropolitan Visiting and Relief Association established. Mid-Victorian example of a local welfare charity.

1844 First Retail Co-operative Society set up in Rochdale.

1859 Publication of Samuel Smiles' *Self-Help*. Outlines the philosophy underlining many Victorian attitudes to poverty and welfare.

1869 Foundation of the Charity Organisation Society. Attempted to control the distribution of charity so that it encouraged independence and self-help.

1870 Local Government Board takes responsibility for the Poor Law. New drive to restrict availability of outdoor relief.

1875 Friendly Societies Act. Attempt to make friendly societies more reliable.

1886 Unemployment crisis. Mansion House fund set up to aid the destitute.

The aim of the 1834 Poor Law Amendment Act was to limit the amount of welfare provided by the State, by making it available only to those who would accept life in the workhouse. The whole thrust of the New Poor Law was to force people to find other ways of protecting themselves against the disasters that life might throw at them, such as unemployment, sickness or the death of a wage earner. As a result, many people who found themselves in poverty, or threatened by it, turned to a wide variety of alternative welfare agencies in times of hardship. Before 1834, the Poor Law was available to give financial support if help from family and friends was not enough. After 1834, only the most desperate would choose this option. People were forced to turn to other forms of welfare in times of hardship. Those who had the resources to do so joined friendly societies or trade union welfare schemes. Charity was another possible source of support. At a local level, family, friends and relatives became even more important as providers of aid and assistance in time of need.

The growth of charitable and self-help institutions was a significant feature of nineteenth-century social history. The historian F.M.L. Thompson writes that,

> 1   The closest the Victorians came to having an apparatus of social services was not, as has frequently been suggested, the result of legislation and official action and through the Poor Laws and support for education, but the consequence of the largely unsystematic efforts of vast numbers of
> 5   individuals and voluntary organisations, mainly inspired by religious motives, and sustained by the work of armies of middle class women.[1]

Historians disagree about the role which these institutions and ideologies played in nineteenth-century society. For example, were charities a genuine response by the wealthy to the hardship they saw around them, or were they a means by which the poor could be forced to adopt middle-class values and attitudes?

1   The Ideas of Self-Help and Charity

> **KEY ISSUES**   What was 'self-help'? What was new about charity in the nineteenth century?

The idea that people should help themselves rather than rely on the State for welfare was the basis of the 1834 Poor Law Amendment Act. People were forced to make other arrangements for dealing with poverty if they wanted to avoid the threat of the workhouse. In 1859 Samuel Smiles' book *Self-Help* was published. The book was a best seller, which suggests that the idea of self-help had become widely accepted. In some ways the idea of helping yourself could be seen as a justification of the capitalist system, which had allowed individuals to accumulate wealth with little regard for their more unfortunate neighbours. For the prosperous Victorian middle classes the idea of self-help was convenient. It suggested that their own position was morally justified because anyone, no matter how humble, could help themselves to rise up to a position of prosperity. It also absolved them from the duty of funding the poor through higher taxes because it implied that poverty was the fault of the individual and only their own efforts could relieve their condition. In *Self-Help*, Samuel Smiles wrote that,

> 1   'Heaven helps those who help themselves' is a well-tried maxim, embodying in a small compass the results of vast human experience. The spirit of self-help is the root of all genuine growth in the individual; and, exhibited in the lives of many, it constitutes the true course of national
> 5   vigour and strength. Help from without is often enfeebling in its effects, but help from within invariably invigorates. Whatever is done for men or classes, to a certain extent takes away the stimulus and necessity of

doing for themselves; and where men are subjected to over-guidance and over-government, the inevitable tendency is to render them
10 comparatively helpless.

But there was also a sense in which self-help encouraged collective action rather than just individual ambition. In the 1866 edition of *Self-Help*, Smiles made the point that, 'the duty of helping one's self in the highest sense involves the helping of one's neighbours' and he praised the work of friendly societies and mutual-aid associations. So far as working-class people were concerned, self-help could be a hymn of praise to individual effort or an encouragement to co-operative support and solidarity. The latter interpretation provided a foundation for the growth of friendly societies, trades unions and co-operatives in the second half of the nineteenth century.

While the philosophy of self-help in its Victorian form was relatively new, ideas of philanthropy and charity were much older. Most societies have a tradition of giving, and the practice of the rich giving to the poor had deep roots in English society. Before the industrial revolution, charitable giving had been one way of building a connection between the classes and keeping the poor to some extent grateful and deferential to the rich.

In the nineteenth century charitable giving was still a way in which the wealthy could gain prestige and status. But charity increasingly took on another function. Groups like the Charity Organisation Society (COS) began to insist that charity had a moral purpose. Charity was to be given to the poor only on the condition that they accept the values of thrift and self-help. People often resented the attempt to impose 'respectable' middle-class forms of behaviour which might be difficult to observe in impoverished circumstances. Some, who accepted the values of self-help, also began to feel that accepting charity was a sign of failure. Working-class accounts of life in this period frequently report individuals who were 'too proud' to accept charity. Other poor people were prepared to go along with the expectations of philanthropists and charity visitors in order to boost their meagre finances. Those in desperate need had little choice but to accept charity if they wanted to survive. However, many were also well aware that the aim of the donors was to change their behaviour. Groups like the Charity Organisation Society which linked charity to moral improvement could be unpopular in working-class communities even if the resources they controlled were in desperate need.

2 Charity

> **KEY ISSUES** What were the different types of charity and philanthropy? How did groups like the COS attempt to regulate charity? Were they successful?

a) The Extent of Charity

It is difficult to quantify precisely the volume of charitable giving in nineteenth-century Britain. Many donations, such as a casual act of generosity to a beggar on the street, went unrecorded, and the accounting records of charities were often poorly kept. However, the statistical evidence that does exist, along with the weight of contemporary opinion, suggest that a massive and growing volume of charity developed in the second half of the century. Across the country thousands of endowed charities and trusts disbursed small amounts of money in their local communities. The Report of the Royal Commission into the Poor Laws of 1909 estimated that the gross income of the endowed charities was just under £1 million, of which two thirds went to groups of people specified in the particular charity's rules (e.g. local elderly people) and one third to the poor generally. Sir Henry Longley, the chief charity commissioner, had estimated similar figures in 1895. London-based charities were particularly impressive. William F. Howe in his 'Classified Directory' produced regular surveys of 700-800 London charities out of the thousand or so of which he was aware. Excluding Missionary and Bible Societies, Howe estimated the income of the London charities in his survey to have been £2,250,000 in 1874-75 rising to £3,150,000 in 1893-94. By way of comparison, the national expenditure of the Poor Law authorities in 1893 was £9,218,000. Many historians of charity such as F.K. Prochaska have repeated the claim that charitable expenditure on the poor far exceeded State expenditure on poor relief in the late nineteenth and early twentieth centuries.[2] However, only a fraction of charitable donations ended up in the pockets of the poor, for they included an array of diverse good causes. Nonetheless the biggest beneficiaries of this generosity were medical charities, and poor people relied on these in times of illness. The frequency with which charity is referred to in contemporary accounts leaves little doubt that it was a significant feature of Victorian society. *The Times* in 1885 claimed that the receipts of philanthropic charities in London were greater than the budgets of several European governments.

b) Middle Class Philanthropy

Those who had become wealthy through the expansion of trade and commerce held the major resources which charities required. Giving to charity became a symbol of Victorian respectability and middle-class families were expected to contribute. Indeed, one study of middle-class households in 1896 revealed that on average these families spent a larger share of their income on charity than on any other item in their budget except food.

General charities for the aid of the poor could be national or local, sometimes established to deal with a temporary crisis or sometimes set up as permanent institutions. For example, the Metropolitan Visiting and Relief Association was founded in 1843 to deal with destitution in London and raised £20,000 in its first year. Between 1860 and 1886 the middle classes responded to distress amongst the London poor by establishing three Mansion House Funds under the patronage of the Lord Mayor of London. In total, these funds raised £135,000. On a national scale, Queen Alexandra's appeal for the relief of distress raised £750,000 in 1905.

Philanthropic employers were sometimes prepared to divert a proportion of their profits to the welfare of their workers. Some of the most famous examples include the mill owner Sir Titus Salt in Bradford, the chocolate manufacturer Cadbury in Birmingham and the soap magnate William Lever on Merseyside. Each of these employers built houses for their workers with good facilities and provided a range of welfare services. Welfare provision for the employees at Colman's Mustard factory in Norwich were supervised by Caroline Colman, the proprietor's wife, and included a sickness benefit society, a clothing club, medical facilities and blanket and parcel distributions for the needy. Beneficial though these improvements were, they could also be seen as a way of keeping workers productive and tied to their job. Many workers found living in a 'company town' oppressive. The owners often interfered in the life of their employees outside the hours of work, often in day to day affairs. For instance, Titus Salt apparently objected to washing lines, which he found unsightly. He banned the inhabitants of his manufacturing community, Saltaire, from using them. Salt apparently rode his horse around this Bradford neighbourhood cutting down the washing of those employees who defied him on this issue. On a more serious level, the penalty for a worker who lost their job could include the loss of home and benefits.

Employer philanthropists usually limited their welfare provision to members of their own workforce. The so-called Five Per Cent Philanthropists who engaged in the provision of housing for the working classes cast their net wider. George Peabody's Housing Trust and Sir Sidney Waterlow's Improved Industrial Dwellings Company both limited their shareholders' profits to five per cent in order to keep down rents to affordable levels. The housing philanthropists did help to improve the lives of their tenants at a time when the idea of State provided council housing was in its infancy. Yet by 1900 seven of the largest trusts and companies still housed fewer than 80,000 people in London, where the greatest need and the greatest effort were concentrated. 'Casual' workers, without regular incomes, were also excluded from philanthropic housing, as regularity of rent paying was deemed essential. Rent was not the only condition of tenancy. The housing philanthropist Octavia Hill took on the management of run-down East End properties on behalf of the land-lord. Hill was explicit about the social changes she expected from those under her control. She was convinced that it was the habits of the poor which drove them into destitution and she provided accom-modation only on the strict condition that her tenants behaved in the way she prescribed:

1 On what principles was I to rule these people? On the same that I had already tried ... with success in other places ... firstly, to demand a strict fulfilment of their duties to me, one of the chief of which would be the punctual payment of rent; and secondly, to endeavour to be so
5 unfailingly just and patient, that they should learn to trust the rule that was over them ... I would make a few improvements at once ... but, for the most part, improvements should be made by degrees, as the people became more capable of valuing and not abusing them.

Octavia Hill was a pioneer in the techniques of housing management and social case work. She was convinced that she could help the destitute escape from poverty by working with them to modify their lifestyles. In her view poverty was the result of individual failings rather than the consequence of social and economic circumstances. Hill was also a prominent member of another organisation which explicitly made improved behaviour a condition for the receipt of philanthropy: the Charity Organisation Society.

c) The Charity Organisation Society

The Charity Organisation Society (COS) was founded in 1869. Its aim was to regulate and organise existing charities so that support given to the poor would be distributed on strict lines. The core of COS philos-ophy was the belief that indiscriminate charity would inevitably demoralise the poor in just the same way as the Old Poor Law was said to have done. Just as its critics believed that the Speenhamland system undermined hard work and independence, so, in the eyes of the COS, unregulated charity would encourage the poor to become idlers and beggars rather than 'respectable' and independent citizens. Conversely, the COS predicted that charitable support given in a specific way to deserving cases would help them to become indepen-dent once more. This was an age when many organisations and indi-viduals sought to base their actions on 'scientific' lines. The COS believed that their principles were based on the science of society, or 'social science'. As part of this scientific approach, they also adopted a research procedure in order to inform their work. The method adopted was that of investigation: a COS volunteer would conduct a close examination of the lifestyles of those applying for help in order to determine whether or not their case was a worthy one.

The establishment of the COS coincided with the new efforts of central government to reduce spending on outdoor relief after 1870. Both the Local Government Board (which from 1870 was responsible for the Poor Law) and the COS shared the view that the 'undeserving' poor (i.e. those who were believed to have brought about their own poverty through their moral failings) should be given only the option of the workhouse. The 'deserving' poor on the other hand, who had fallen on hard times through no fault of their own, could be offered limited charity to help them get back on their feet. The COS hoped that charities in each area would adopt procedures like the Birmingham ticket system. Here charity givers would give applicants a ticket which they would then take along to the local COS office. Following a rigorous enquiry into their circumstances, the applicant would then take the ticket containing the result of the investigation back to the originating charity. Depending on the outcome they would be given help or sent away. The basis on which COS visitors would make such decisions is indicated by the guidelines of the Southampton COS. These recommended:

> the rejection of undeserving drunkards and incorrigible idlers; those who were careless and improvident ... and those who were in an absolute state of destitution fit only for the workhouse.

Charitable aid was to be given only to those who would benefit, morally as well as materially, from the help they were given. Relief was always to be temporary, personal and designed to reform the habits of the individual concerned. It was to be part of a plan for the permanent benefit of the recipient.

The COS was a powerful institution in the 1870s and 1880s and was supported by key figures from the ruling elite. The 54 strong inaugural council who met in London in 1869 included people from the hierarchies of Parliament, the aristocracy, the established church, banking, the professions and the armed forces. In the 1870s, the COS had 24 vice-presidents including dukes, earls, viscounts and leading public figures. The organisation's propaganda emphasised its success in working with the new strict Poor Law and in weeding out 'scroungers' and its ability to target relief at those who deserved it. Yet the success of the COS in imposing its hard-line approach to charity is questionable. Outside London, provincial COS branches often failed to recruit enough volunteers or raise adequate funds. This meant that they were unable to regulate charitable relief. Relationships with local Poor Law Boards of Guardians were frequently strained as COS branches trespassed into Poor Law territory or criticised local unions for their relief policies. Old and new charities alike were reluctant to give up their right to decide how to spend their money to the COS 'charity police'. Many charities, especially those run by evangelical Christians, opposed the lack of compassion inherent in the COS's 'scientific principles'.

One historian of the COS, Robert Humphreys, has noted that, 'most outsiders saw their technique as an obsession with probing and prying into poor people's personal affairs'.[3] There was a strong smack of social authoritarianism in the COS approach to poverty and welfare. Even in the late nineteenth century not everyone was prepared to go along with this. Much charity continued to be disbursed in an indiscriminate way, despite the objections of the COS and its supporters. The 1886 Mansion House fund, which was set up to relieve distress in London, drew stinging criticism from the COS which alleged that the fund was being distributed without proper regard to the circumstances of the recipients. Despite these objections, the fund still raised £80,000. However, even though it failed to live up to its own publicity, there is little doubt that the COS did have a major influence on the way charities operated. Those seeking help were more often than not forced to package their requests in terms which emphasised that their case was deserving in the eyes of the philanthropists.

d) How the Poor Responded to Charity

Under the influence of the COS, many poor people looking for charitable relief had to consider the sensibilities and respectable concerns of the charity givers as well as the nature of their own needs. Church-based charities, for example, would expect children to attend Sunday schools if they were providing relief for a family in their parish. Evidence of drinking or any other luxury had to be hidden by the supplicants and any hint of charity-mongering - making applications to lots of different charities - was frowned upon. Poor people seeking charity were therefore involved in a battle of wits with the charity providers. The front-line troops on the other side of this battle were the charity 'visitors', the small army of up to half a million mainly female middle-class volunteers who made the decisions as to who should, or should not, receive aid.

Literature from the period often suggests that respectable working people shunned charity in order to emphasise their independence. Certainly the stigma attached to much charity encouraged this attitude. Many poor people were also resistant to the imposition of 'middle class' values as the price to be paid for rather meagre handouts. However, recent research into the lifestyles of the poor has revealed a complex set of relationships and attitudes regarding the use of charity in this period. Historians now pay more attention to the crucial role of women in managing the households of working-class families.[4] Although the male wage was often crucial to family survival, so were the casual earnings of women workers. The expenditure and

A Church of England charity poster, 1892

management decisions of the housewife were no less vital in making ends meet. Women had to maximise the alternative sources of income in order to eke out a living in late-Victorian cities. Women in poor households could not afford to neglect the opportunities for supplementary support provided by the charities. For example, the COS condemned the provision of free meals by charity, suggesting that it undermined the role of the mother. Nevertheless, 52,000 London children were sent to get free meals provided by charities in 1895. Sometimes these meals were provided in ways which did seek to stigmatise the families concerned, but they were too valuable a resource to turn down.

Mothers trying to raise families in conditions of poverty really needed extra cash to boost the household revenue, but this was rarely provided by the philanthropists. Charities preferred to supply relief in kind such as boots, clothing and meals for children or coal for the fire. In this way they hoped that the gift would be used in the way in which they decided, rather than in the way which the recipient might actually want. But there were ways round this. Sturdy middle-class children's clothing provided by charities could be sold or put into the pawnshop in order to provide immediate cash. Coal tickets could be sold on to generate extra income and even the bread and butter available at free meal halls could be stashed away for use by other family members. Much of this might seem petty but for people living on the margins of survival and starvation every little helped. The stories of how poor families coped throw light on the ingenuity and creativity with which they made best use of the little welfare that was available and attempted to use it on their own terms rather than those of the charity providers.

3 Working Class Self-Help

> **KEY ISSUE** How successful were friendly societies, trade unions, co-operatives and poor communities in providing welfare for the poor?

a) Friendly Societies and Burial Societies

Friendly societies began when groups of neighbours, friends or workmates decided to form an association to protect themselves in time of need. Each member would contribute a certain amount of money each week and in return they would be entitled to payments from the funds if they found themselves in need due to sickness, unemployment or bereavement. Early friendly societies were small scale so that the members could feel that they had direct control over the association and they would meet on a regular basis, usually in a pub, to discuss the affairs of the organisation. The attraction of such a democratic and sociable form of welfare protection led to a big expansion of friendly societies at the start of the nineteenth century; workers particularly needed to insure themselves against the uncertainties of life thrown up by the industrial revolution and so the greatest increases in friendly society membership around 1800 were in rapidly industrialising and urbanising areas, such as Lancashire. Total membership grew from 704,000 in 1803 to 925,000 in 1815.

Despite initial concerns that the friendly societies might be covers for seditious and revolutionary organisation, middle and upper-class opinion in the early nineteenth century came to support these working class associations, as it was hoped that self-help would provide an alternative to the Poor Law and keep the poor rates down. However, both the authorities and the members themselves became concerned at some of the problems that the early friendly societies were facing. The biggest problem was that the societies had no accurate way of knowing how much they should pay out in benefits. If they were too cautious the members would feel they were getting a raw deal, but if they were too generous the society could easily go bankrupt. As the century progressed, actuarial tables allowing associations and insurance companies to predict viable levels of subscriptions and payments became increasingly sophisticated, but in the 1820s they were still in their infancy. Government Acts of 1819 and 1829 attempted to give the better societies a hallmark of respectability by allowing them to become registered if they fulfilled certain conditions, such as submitting rules and accounts. Nevertheless, even some registered societies continued to fail and when this happened the members stood to lose all the money they had paid in.

One way to reduce the risk of failure was to expand the size of the friendly society. It was hoped that a big association with thousands of members and large funds would be able to withstand short-term financial crises, such as trade depressions, which would destroy a smaller association. Another attraction of a large organisation was that it could be nationwide so that members would not be forced to leave the society if they moved to another part of the country. Friendly societies with large numbers of affiliated branches throughout the country began to grow in the 1830s and 1840s. Undoubtedly, the introduction of the New Poor Law in 1834 was a significant cause of this expansion as workers sought to protect themselves from the workhouse system. Of the 3,074 affiliated lodges of the Manchester Unity of Oddfellows (the biggest affiliated friendly society) still active in 1870, nearly half (1,407) were founded in the decade after the 1834 Act.

As real wages rose in the middle of the nineteenth century, so the friendly societies continued to expand. By 1872 there were 34 affiliated societies with over one thousand members each. The figures for the two biggest societies, the Manchester Unity of Oddfellows and the Ancient Order of Foresters, illustrate the extent of this growth:

Year	Manchester Unity of Oddfellows	Ancient Order of Foresters
1850	224,878	80,089
1870	434,100	361,735
1899	713,000	666,000

Members of these affiliated societies would pay a few pennies a week in return for 8 to 10 shillings per week sickness benefit, payment of doctor's fees, and a funeral grant of up to £10. 'Tramping allowances' were also paid to allow members to travel in search of work. For many people however, even 5d. or 6d. a week was more than they could afford. For them, Burial Societies were a cheaper alternative.

Death in the family was a major cost that people needed some insurance against. However, it was the shame of a pauper funeral which was the chief motivation behind the growth of burial societies. If poor people had little else, they at least wanted the dignity of a proper send off when they died. The early burial societies were rather like the early friendly societies in that they were small, local affairs which were under the control of their members. As the name suggests, they were a very limited form of welfare protection as they only paid death benefits. The Blackburn Philanthropic Burial Society, for example, provided a burial allowance of £4 or £5 in return for a payment of 1d. or 1½d per week. There was generally no provision for sickness benefit. Although many of the local burial societies continued to operate, the market soon became dominated by a small number of large societies which had expanded rapidly: the Royal Liver Society, which had been formed by Liverpool workers in 1850, already had a membership of 550,000 by 1870. Between them the Royal Liver, the Liverpool Victoria Legal and the Royal London had over six million members by 1905. The Royal Liver provided the option of sickness payments as well, but most of its members were too poor to pay the increased contributions necessary for this benefit. Indeed these large 'collecting' societies (so called because they relied on an army of part-time collectors to gather in the weekly contributions) concentrated their efforts on the poorest part of the population.

The scale of these working class self-help institutions in the late nineteenth century is impressive: it is probable that a majority of working class people had some form of friendly society protection by 1900. However, as an alternative form of social welfare provision, this kind of working class self-help was severely restricted. Membership of friendly societies was inevitably limited to better paid workers and the poorest were actively excluded. Despite the fact that both the Manchester Unity of Oddfellows and the Ancient Order of Foresters had some success in recruiting agricultural labourers in the 1860s and 1870s, workers in low paid jobs generally found it impossible to pay the contributions necessary to gain sickness benefit. To a family living on about £1 a week income, every penny counted in the struggle for survival and even 6d. per week would be more than they could afford. The poorest sections of the population also suffered from irregularity of employment: work might be seasonal or income might vary from week to week. In these circumstances it was virtually impossible to keep up the regular weekly payments necessary to guarantee sickness protection. Moreover, societies often fined members who missed out on their weekly payment. Some friendly societies refused membership to applicants who were regarded as 'high risk'. Those with a history of illness, those who were over 40 or those who were in dangerous occupations such as mining were excluded. Nearly all societies charged an entrance fee and this would be another significant barrier to the poor, who could little afford to save money for such a purpose.

Even for those who did manage to join a friendly society, there was no guarantee that it would provide for them in times of need. Despite a Royal Commission on friendly societies in the 1870s and numerous Acts of Parliament, societies continued to collapse or fail to look after their members. The United Assurance Society collapsed in 1885 leaving its 148,627 members stranded. There had been a public enquiry into the operation of the Royal Liver Friendly Society in 1884. This revealed that those running the society were making a very good living at the expense of the poor who were its members, and resulted in the resignation of the two secretaries. Other societies were also attacked for the high costs of their management. It is also clear that the large collecting societies were quite cynical in the way that they encouraged people to join up in the full knowledge that they would be unlikely to be able to keep up their payments. In 1905 alone the Royal Liver reported that 47,000 memberships had been terminated on death but 682,000 other memberships had lapsed from other causes. It can only be assumed that the majority of these people failed to keep up their payments and, as a result, lost all that they had previously contributed.

As an alternative to the workhouse, the majority of the population would certainly have preferred to have been covered by a friendly society. However, the poorest were effectively denied this option and even those who could afford the higher levels of contribution necessary for sick benefit could still find themselves in need in old age. While some societies did provide for their elderly members it was generally too expensive an undertaking. Both the Oddfellows and the Foresters introduced pensions schemes in the 1890s but the take-up was low due to the high cost. For many, friendly societies and burial societies provided some form of alternative welfare provision, but for others it was an inadequate alternative. A survey of adult male workhouse inmates in 1881 found that 11,304 had once been members of friendly societies. Of these, 7,391 had failed to keep up their contributions and the other 3,913 had been members of societies which had collapsed.

b) Trade Unions and Co-operatives

Like the friendly societies, the trade union movement expanded in the mid to late nineteenth century. Insofar as the purpose of trade unions was to negotiate for higher pay for their members, these working class institutions made an important contribution to raising the standard of living of their members. However, as with friendly societies, membership of trade unions in the mid-nineteenth century tended to be concentrated amongst skilled and relatively prosperous workers, such as the engineers and the carpenters. Some of these 'new model' unions could provide good levels of welfare for their members. The Amalgamated Society of Carpenters provided out-of-work benefit of 15s per week and sickness benefit of 12s. per week for up to 26 weeks, reducing to 6s. per week thereafter. Members were also entitled to £12 funeral benefit, accident benefit of up to £100 and a pension of between 5s. and 8s. per week depending on how long the individual had belonged to the union. Only well-paid workers like the carpenters could afford the 1s. per week subscription required to finance this scheme and membership of the union was only 8,261 in 1867. Even other unions of skilled workers such as the Brickmakers Society of London had no sickness fund like that of the carpenters. The big unions of unskilled workers, which were formed in the 1880s and 1890s, were simply unable to provide the kind of benefits offered by the carpenters' union because their low paid members could not

A Co-operative Society poster, circa 1898

afford to pay such high subscriptions. Instead, they concentrated on using their funds to improve pay and conditions by financing strikes, rather than providing welfare schemes.

The Co-operative movement was yet another impressive example of working-class self-help which nevertheless provided no alternative welfare system. Co-operative shops were owned by their members and returned all their surplus profits to the membership by way of dividends. By 1891 there were a million co-op shareholders. As with the friendly societies and the new model trade unions, retail co-operatives provided for the more skilled sections of the working class, or at least those who were in regular employment. Co-operative shops did try to look after their members in times of depression and during industrial disputes. Co-operative activity also extended to friendly society type activities, such as funeral provision. However, retail co-operatives had a strict rule about not providing credit and for the poorest sections of the population buying now and paying later was an essential survival strategy. Co-op dividends were also based on the amount spent by customers. Consequently those who had least to spend received the lowest dividends.

c) Family, Friends and Neighbours

While the institutional manifestations of working-class self-help, such as friendly societies, trade unions and co-operatives, seem to have often by-passed the really poor, mutual aid and support of a more informal nature was central to the lives of the poor in Victorian Britain. Contemporaries frequently regarded the poor in the cities as being brutalised by their poverty and unable to do anything to help themselves. Writers at the time used terms such as 'the abyss' to describe the poorest working class neighbourhoods and their inhabitants were depicted as a tribe of semi-wild savages who were beyond civilisation. In 1890 General William Booth, the founder of the Salvation Army, published a book entitled *In Darkest England and the Way Out*. The title deliberately tried to parallel the European exploration of 'darkest Africa' which was going on at the same time.

Just as the inhabitants of 'darkest Africa' had their own culture and lifestyle, even if Victorian explorers did not always recognise it, so the inhabitants of the worst inner-city slums also developed a way of life which helped them to cope with the environment in which they found themselves. At the time, the sheer scale of the poverty and misery often blinded observers to the many ways in which the poor supported each other in order to survive.[5] This is not to deny the cruelty, crime and degradation that did exist, but historians are now uncovering the complexity of life in poor nineteenth-century neighbourhoods in a more sympathetic fashion. Research into the most notorious areas, such as St. Giles in London or Summer Lane in Birmingham, has revealed that the poor provided each other with a great deal of welfare in the absence of help from other institutions. Overcrowding in Victorian courts and slums meant that it was impossible for people to lead isolated existences. There was very little private space and people would inevitably have intimate knowledge of each other's business. This meant helping out when your neighbour was in particular need. The presence of a large number of kin from the same families or migrants from the same area further strengthened local networks. According to the historian Lynn Lees.

> 1 Irish neighbours contributed money for funeral expenses, if the dead person's kin could not raise enough. Neighbours loaned money and kitchen utensils, helped orphans to find jobs and lodging, attended wakes and weddings. Newcomers were given a corner of a room in which to
> 5 sleep and helped in their search for work.[6]

Working class autobiographies from the period reveal a high level of support and generosity in the midst of great poverty, as illustrated by the oral testimony of a woman born in Hackney in 1903:

> 1 And mother used to say to me, 'Poor Mrs. Somebody next door. She's got no food in the house.' So mother used to have a good old nourishing stew, and she used to cook it in a big saucepan with handles on both sides. And I was the one to take it in to Mrs. Somebody next door. And
> 5 she'd say 'Oh, thank you ever so much!' and she used to feed the kids.

Even some contemporaries acknowledged this mutual support. For example, the Rev. William Conybeare, writing about the poor in south London in 1908, commented that, 'The poor breathe an atmosphere of charity. They cannot understand life without it. And it is largely this kindness of the poor to the poor which stands between our civilisation and revolution.' The journalist George Sims in his 1883 report entitled *How the Poor Live* noted that charitable giving, even at the cost of great hardship to the giver, was common amongst the poor. In his 1889 work *Horrible London* he expanded on this point:

> 1 The poor are kinder to each other than the rich; they are bound by stronger ties of sympathy; their hearts respond more readily to generous impulses. They have greater opportunities of helping each other, and there are no barriers of pride between them. They live their
> 5 lives before each others' eyes, and their joys and sorrows are the common property of the entire community.

Mutual help and welfare in the poorest areas could come in a variety of forms. Easy access to child care arrangements was particularly important in communities where casual opportunities of work might appear unpredictably. There is much evidence that the task of looking after children was shared by the women of poor neighbourhoods. Money transactions were also frequent: people would lend to others when there was a crisis and borrow when they were in need. Families would feed each others' children and lend each other food. Clothing, especially children's clothing, would be circulated through the community. People would take care of sick and elderly neighbours and friends, rather than see them consigned to the workhouse. People would look out for work for family and neighbours newly arrived in the area and provide them with somewhere to stay, despite intolerable levels of overcrowding. People might not be members of friendly societies or burial clubs, but neighbours would collect money to pay for funeral expenses when necessary. None of this represented a substitute for a proper welfare system, but these networks of support were in many cases the primary ways in which survival was possible for the poorest Victorians and Edwardians.

4 Historical Interpretations of Charity and Self-Help

> **KEY ISSUES** Did charity and self-help contribute to the prosperity of the working class or was it a means by which the middle class maintained their control over society?

Historians have debated the purposes behind the huge amount of charity and philanthropy that existed in the nineteenth century. Some historians believe that the philanthropists had a genuine concern to deal with the poverty they saw around them in order to improve society. F.K. Prochaska, for example, characterises charity and philanthropy as natural extensions of the 'kindness' that individuals will show to one another in any society.[7] Brian Harrison also sees philanthropy in a positive light. He argues that it created bonds which brought the working and middle classes together. It also created a consensus within which the respectable working classes could join with the middle classes in their disapproval of the 'undeserving' poor.[8]

These views represent a reaction to the theory of 'social control' which was put forward in the 1970s by historians such as A.P. Donajgrodski and Gareth Stedman Jones.[9] This theory held that the middle classes were able to maintain their wealth and power in nineteenth-century Britain not just by the exercise of force (such as crushing strikes and working-class protest movements like the Chartists) but also by imposing their own ideas and values onto the working classes, so that they would accept their exploitation as a legitimate thing. Supporters of the social control theory argue that philanthropists and charities were not simply motivated by good intentions. They point to the COS as a classic example of an organisation dedicated to reforming working class manners and values, so that they conformed with middle-class expectations.

Friendly societies and trade unions have also been attacked by the advocates of social control theory. These institutions are seen as accepting the values of the middle classes, rather than fighting to change the system itself. By supporting the idea that working people could look after themselves and prosper within capitalism, friendly societies and 'new model' trade unions implicitly condemned the poor who failed to do this. Moreover, by providing, along with philanthropy, an alternative welfare system, these institutions actually set back the cause of welfare reform by the State. Other historians of the left, even if they accept elements of the social control argument, believe that working-class self-help represented a heroic and practical solution to the problems people faced. They argue that these collective approaches to poverty formed the foundations for the struggle to provide collective welfare through the State.

The American conservative historian Gertrude Himmelfarb is another critic of the theory of social control. She has argued that the values which the COS and others encouraged were the values of the working class just as much as the middle class. She asks,

> If thrift, prudence, sobriety, industry, cleanliness and independence were middle-class values, is it to be assumed that drunkenness, idleness, dirtiness, and dependency were indigenous working-class values?[10]

Certainly closer examination of poor communities has revealed that the values and lifestyles of their populations were varied and complex. Many liberal and left-wing historians now modify the simple social control theory by acknowledging that the mutual support in these communities was based on the needs of the people rather than the values of the middle-class. Nevertheless, they would still hold the view that certain beliefs and behaviours served to support the capitalist system and, although the adoption of these values might help some individuals to improve their circumstances, it was the system which created their poverty in the first place.

Historians will continue to hold different views regarding the role of the voluntary sector in the provision of welfare in the nineteenth century. Modern debates about how far the State should be responsible for welfare provision and how far this should be left up to individuals and institutions, clearly have an impact on historical interpretations. Few historians now put forward the social control theory without extensive modifications. Yet there is no doubt that self-help and *laissez-faire* values did suit the economic interests of the middle classes much more than the working class. This is not to deny that philanthropists and friendly societies did provide genuine and needed support. But despite their efforts, one thing remains clear: a significant percentage of the population at the bottom of the social structure had needs which were barely, if at all, met by either philanthropy or organised self-help bodies. It was the plight of this 'residuum' which began to fascinate social observers in the second half of the 1800s.

References

1   F.M.L. Thompson, *The Rise of Respectable Society* (Fontana, 1989), p 252.
2   F.K. Prochaska, *Philanthropy* in F.M.L. Thompson (ed.), *Cambridge Social History of Britain 1750-1950*, Vol. 3 (Cambridge, 1993), Ch. 7.
3   Robert Humphreys, *Sin, Organized Charity and the Poor Law in Victorian Britain* (St. Martin's Press, 1995), Ch. 6.
4   For example, Ellen Ross, *Hungry Children: Housewives and London Charity, 1870-1918*, in Peter Mandler (ed.), *The Uses of Charity: The Poor on Relief in the Nineteenth Century Metropolis* (University of Pennsylvania Press, 1990), Ch. 6.
5   For example, Jerry White, *Rothschild Buildings: Life in an East End Tenement Block* (1980), and Martin Daunton (ed.), *Charity, Self interest and Welfare in the English Past* (UCL Press, 1996).
6   Lynn Lees, *Exiles of Erin* (Manchester University Press, 1979), p. 83, quoted in Anna Davin, *Growing Up Poor* (Rivers Oram, 1996).
7   F.K. Prochaska, *The Voluntary Impulse* (London, 1988).
8   Brian Harrison, *Peaceable kingdom: stability and change in modern Britain* (Oxford, 1983).
9   A.P. Donajgrodski, *Social Control in Nineteenth Century Britain* (Croom Helm, 1977); G. Stedman Jones, *Outcast London: a study in the relationship between classes in Victorian society* (Oxford, 1971).
10 G. Himmelfarb, *Poverty and Compassion* (Vintage, 1992), p. 201.

Working on Chapter 4

This is a complex area covering ideas, institutions and attitudes. When making notes on the chapter try to look at each alternative to the Poor Law in three ways: firstly, the ideas underpinning the particular source of welfare; secondly, the institution or group itself; thirdly, the impact it had on poverty. The diagram on page 78 will help you to clarify the key areas.

Source-based questions on Chapter 4

1. Self-help
Read the extracts from Samuel Smiles on pages 60-61, Lynn Lees on page 74 and the Southampton COS on page 65.

a) Explain what Smiles meant by 'Self-help'. (2 marks)
b) Why did Smiles believe that government intervention was undesirable? (2 marks)
c) What are the differences between the self-help described in the extract on page 74 and the view of the Southampton COS on page 65? (4 marks)

2. Philanthropy and charity
Read the extracts from Octavia Hill on page 64 and the Southampton COS on page 65.

a) On what principles did Octavia Hill manage her tenants? (2 marks)
b) What criticisms could be made of Hill's approach? (2 marks)
c) How far were Hill's principles similar to those of the Southampton COS? (4 marks)

3. Co-operation and charity
Look at the posters on pages 67 and 72.

a) What message is the Co-operative Society poster trying to convey? (2 marks)
b) To what extent is the poster from the Church of England Central Society attempting to convey a similar message? (6 marks)

4. Neighbourhood support networks
Read the extracts on page 74 from George Sims, from the woman in Hackney, and on the Irish.

a) What do the three sources tell us about working-class support networks in poor communities? (2 marks)
b) Does the evidence from the Hackney woman support the opinion of George Sims on the issue of mutual help and welfare? (4 marks)
c) Is the evidence from the extract on the Irish neighbourhood more or less reliable than the other two extracts? Explain your answer. (4 marks)

Summary Diagram
Charity and Self-help

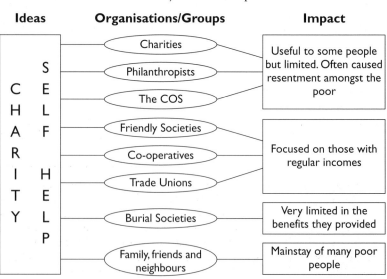

5 Changing Attitudes to Poverty 1850-1900

POINTS TO CONSIDER

This chapter examines the ways in which the problem of poverty was revealed to the wider public in the second half of the nineteenth century. It concerns attitudes, and the way they can change. On your first reading of the chapter try to establish what the dominant ideas about poverty were in the mid-nineteenth century. Then, examine the main writers covered in this chapter. List the ways in which the writings of Mayhew, Booth and Rowntree challenged these ideas and the other developments that supported this challenge. Try to see how these new writings also suggested a more active role for the State in the provision of welfare.

KEY DATES

1850-52 Henry Mayhew publishes *London Labour and the London Poor* in a series of pamphlets.

1851 Great Exhibition. Celebration of British industrial wealth and supremacy.

1852 Publication of Charles Dickens' *Bleak House*.

1875 Public Health Act. Local authorities forced to improve sanitary conditions.

1870 Education Act. Beginning of State-controlled education system.

1889 Publication of first volume of Charles Booth's *Life and Labour of the People in London.*

1901 Publication of Seebohm Rowntree's *Poverty: A Study of Town Life.*

1 Introduction

KEY ISSUES What were the three dominant ideas about poverty in the mid-nineteenth century and how were they challenged after 1850?

Attitudes to poverty in the first half of the nineteenth century were dominated by three ideas. Firstly, it was believed that poverty was caused by the personal failure of the individual concerned. Laziness, drunkenness and extravagance were seen to be the causes of hardship. Secondly, it was assumed that anyone could help themselves out of poverty by adopting the values of self-help. It was argued that hard work, thrift and sobriety would lead to prosperity and respectability for anyone who followed this ethic. Thirdly, the idea that the government should help to solve poverty by giving the poor more money was seen as disastrous. It was said that government handouts would simply encourage dependency and the poor would have no incentive to help themselves. This was the idea behind the harshness of the New Poor Law. It was also the idea behind the Charity Organisation Society's attack on indiscriminate philanthropy. (See pages 64-66.)

In the second half of the century three new ideas began to challenge the old assumptions. Firstly, writers of many types, including government officials, journalists, novelists and social investigators, began to paint an increasingly distressing picture of the extent of poverty, particularly in the big cities. The poor, it seemed, represented a large proportion of the population - maybe up to a third. Moreover, despite indications that society as a whole was becoming increasingly prosperous, there was little sign that the number of people in poverty was decreasing. Worse still, the horrible depths of poverty and the nightmarish vision of life in the city slums came as a shock to comfortable middle-class opinion. It seemed as if their society was somehow failing.

The second idea exposed by these revelations was that the poor were not necessarily responsible for their own situation. This is not to say that writers stopped commenting on the social and moral failings of the poor. On the contrary, nearly all the most important writers in this period continued in their accounts to find drunkenness, cruelty and criminality amongst the poor. And they continued to condemn these things and highlight them as causes of poverty. However, investigators began to find that some of the poor, perhaps the majority, were not the authors of their own misfortune. Time and again it was revealed that poor people tried to work hard and lead decent lives, but found themselves trapped in circumstances over which they had no control. Unemployment, irregularity of work, low wages, sickness or death were forces largely beyond the control of the individual. This was a challenge to the whole notion of self-help. It also led to the third new proposition. If individuals were indeed victims of social and economic circumstances beyond their control, should not a larger power intervene on their behalf to protect them from the consequences? Despite the attempts of philanthropists and friendly societies, it became clear to many that only the State itself was powerful enough to undertake this role.

It would be misleading to suggest that these changes in attitude came about in a smooth and linear fashion. The *laissez-faire* belief that governments should not interfere in social and economic affairs continued to be held by influential people throughout the century. Indeed the high point of 'individualist' thinking was probably around 1869-70, when the COS was founded and the Poor Law authorities began their 'crusade' against outdoor relief. Social investigators such as Charles Booth remained attached to individualist solutions, even after they had revealed that poverty had causes bigger than the individual. Nevertheless, it is fair to say that as the century drew to its close, a new consensus was beginning to emerge. Individual action was not enough by itself to tackle poverty. Collective solutions were also required.

2 The Representation of the Poor in the Mid-Nineteenth Century

> **KEY ISSUE** How did the representation of the poor by writers such as Mayhew and Dickens challenge the view that poverty was the result of individual moral failure?

a) Henry Mayhew

Henry Mayhew was one of the earliest writers to document the depths of poverty that existed in Victorian London. Mayhew was born in 1812, one of 17 children. Like five of his six brothers, Henry joined his father's law practice, only to abandon this for a career in journalism. He was one of the founders of the satirical magazine *Punch* in July 1841. He co-edited the publication for a few months and continued to contribute to it until 1845. In the late 1840s Mayhew was recruited to the *Morning Chronicle* to act as metropolitan correspondent for their national investigation into labour and the poor. Starting in October 1849, he wrote 83 letters for the *Chronicle*, describing the working and living conditions of the London poor. But, in October 1850, he fell out with the management of the newspaper and started to publish his investigations independently as a series of weekly parts. From late December 1850 until February 1852, Mayhew published 63 twopenny pamphlets under the title *London Labour and the London Poor*. This work, along with some new material, was eventually reproduced as a four-volume book in 1861-62, also under the title *London Labour and the London Poor*.

The full title of Mayhew's four-volume work was *London Labour and the London Poor; A Cyclopaedia of the Condition and Earnings of Those That Will Work, Those That Cannot Work and Those That Will Not Work*. It seems that his original aim was to survey a sample of the whole working population of London, arranged under the sub-headings of the title. However, the first three volumes of *London Labour* in fact only dealt with one particular category of Londoner, 'The London Street-Folk; comprising Street Sellers, Street Buyers, Street Finders, Street Performers, Street Artisans, Street Labourers.' Volume four dealt with 'Those That Will Not Work, comprising Prostitutes, Thieves, Swindlers and Beggars.' The result is that Mayhew's survey concentrated on some of the most precarious and bizarre occupations in the capital, at the expense of those in more regular work. The lives of rat-catchers, pure-finders (collectors of dog excrement which was used to 'purify' leather), sewer-hunters, glass-eye sellers, street sellers of litera-ture (at least 28 different types), costermongers (hundreds of different types), dredgermen, mud-larks, crossing-sweepers, snake-swallowers and an infinite variety of other ways of scraping a living are painstakingly described by Mayhew. He calculated that there were about 50,000, the majority of whom led lives of pitiful wretchedness. What most had in common, despite the variety of their callings, was the marginal and unpredictable nature of their work.

Mayhew's investigations centred on face to face interviews with the subjects of his study. He claimed that he recounted the stories of the people he interviewed exactly as they had told them. He used the literal language and pronunciation of his interviewees and promised his readers that he had added nothing to what they said. The result was a series of extremely powerful accounts conjuring up a world unknown to Mayhew's middle-class readers, an 'undiscovered country of the poor' as he described it. One of his subjects was a ham sand-wich seller:

1　His look and manners were subdued; and, though his dress was old and worn, it was clean and unpatched. 'I hardly remember my father, sir,' he said; 'but I believe, if he'd lived, I should have been better off. My mother couldn't keep my brother and me - he's older than me - when we grew
5　to be twelve or thirteen, and we had to shift for ourselves ... I was first in place as a sort of errand boy, then I was a stationer's boy, and then a news agent's boy. I wasn't wanted any longer, but left with a good char-acter. My brother had gone into the sandwich trade - I hardly knew what made him - and he advised me to be a ham sandwich-man, and so I
10　started as one. At first I made 10s., and 7s., and 8s. a week - that's seven years or so - but things are worse now, and I make 3s. 6d. some weeks, and 5s. others, and 6s. is an out and outer. My rent's 2s. a week, but I haven't my own things. I'm so sick of this life, I'd do anything to get out of it; but I don't see a way ... I do dread the winter so. I've stood up to
15　the ankles in snow till after midnight, and till I've wished I was snow myself, and could melt like it and have an end.... I've often walked eight miles to see if I could find ham a halfpenny a pound cheaper anywhere ... If I was sick there's only the parish for me ...

From cases such as these Mayhew came to a number of conclusions. Firstly, the level of poverty experienced by the street-folk of London was desperate and unacceptable. Secondly, the condition of the street-folk was not necessarily of their own making. Some people might be responsible for their own situation, and Mayhew was willing to condemn the idle. But circumstances were the primary cause of poverty. 'The deserving poor,' he wrote, 'are really those who cannot live by their labour, whether from under-payment, want of employ-ment, or physical or mental incapacity'. His description of the daily scramble for work of casual labourers at the London docks emphasised how reliant people were on forces beyond their control. If the wind blew in the wrong direction, the ships would be delayed and the dockers would starve:

| That the sustenance of thousands of families should be as fickle as the very breeze itself; that the weathercock should be the index of daily want or daily ease to a vast number of men, women and children, was a climax of misery that I could not have imagined to exist.

Thirdly, Mayhew challenged the complacency of his middle-class readership with this reality and threatened an alarming future if nothing was done. Having reminded his readers of the 'truth' that they too could have been in the same predicament but for good fortune and the help of others, Mayhew continued:

| It is the continued forgetfulness of this truth - a truth which our wretched self-conceit is constantly driving from our minds - that prevents our stirring to improve the condition of these poor people; though, if we knew but the whole of the facts concerning them, and their
5 sufferings and feelings, our very fears alone for the safety of the state would be sufficient to make us do something on their behalf. I am quite satisfied, from all I have seen, that there are thousands in this great metropolis ready to rush forth, on the least evidence of a rising of the people, to commit the most savage and revolting excesses

The threat of social revolution by the desperate and dispossessed of London was a powerful way of focusing middle-class attention on the problem of poverty.

Henry Mayhew's work has been attacked by a number of historians. His investigation was erratic and the original plan to survey the whole labouring population collapsed. His concentration on the most marginal workers and his failure to deal with the numerous groups of workers in more regular occupations (e.g. the 168,000 domestic servants) is said to have produced an exaggerated picture of the extent of poverty. Mayhew was a popular journalist who needed to sell his publications to earn a living, and this may have motivated him to present the most dramatic and colourful scene. Some of his characters, such as Jack Black the rat-catcher, were certainly larger than life. The accuracy of Mayhew's work has also been questioned. Some of his interviews may have been staged: there is evidence that particularly interesting 'specimens' of the London poor were brought to his office, where their stories were embellished by Mayhew and his assistants. Many of Mayhew's statistics have also been shown to be unreliable.

Whatever the level of reliability of his work, Mayhew's writing certainly had a major impact on the understanding of poverty. The weekly pamphlets had a circulation of some 13,000 and inspired at least eight imitators and two popular stage plays in the 1850s.

Reviewers in newspapers and magazines praised Mayhew's efforts and expressed their shock and horror at his revelations. William Thackeray summed up the impact of Mayhew:

> 1 ... these wonders and terrors have been lying by your door and mine ever since we had a door of our own. We had but to go a hundred yards off and see for ourselves, but we never did ... Of such wonderous and complicated misery as this you confess you had no idea? No. How
> 5 should you? - you and I - we are of the upper classes; we have had hitherto no community with the poor.

Mayhew revealed a previously hidden world and in describing that world he raised questions about accepted views on poverty and challenged those in authority to respond.

b) Charles Dickens

Charles Dickens was probably the best-selling novelist of the Victorian period. His major works, published in weekly parts, each sold tens and even hundreds of thousands of copies. In the 12 years after his death in 1870, Dickens' books sold four million copies in England alone. They were read by all classes and his characters were more familiar and famous than most living celebrities of the age. His portrayal of poverty and the poor was therefore an important influence on public opinion and on the consciousness of policy-makers. Though he was a journalist and social campaigner as well as a novelist, Dickens' work was not polemical. His intention was to write a good story, and his tales held no consistent view on the problem of poverty or its solution. Nevertheless, Dickens' work did consistently emphasise two points. Firstly, it portrayed the poor as real people who suffered like everyone else. This might not seem like a great achievement but, at a time when the poor were often portrayed as idlers or criminals, if they were portrayed at all, this did help to bring a human dimension to a social problem. In *Bleak House* (1852) Dickens described the 'outcast' life of Jo, the poor crossing sweeper:

> 1 It must be very puzzling to see the good company going to the churches on Sundays, with their books in their hands, and to think (for perhaps Jo does think, at odd times) what does it all mean, and if it means anything to anybody, how comes it that it means nothing to me? To be hustled,
> 5 and jostled, and moved on; and really to feel that it would appear to be perfectly true that I have no business here, or there, or anywhere; and yet to be perplexed by the consideration that I am here somehow, too ... It must be a strange state, not merely to be told that I am scarcely human (as in the case of offering myself as a witness), but to feel it of
> 10 my own knowledge all my life! To see the horses, dogs, and cattle, go by me, and to know that in ignorance I belong to them, and not to the superior beings in my shape, whose delicacy I offend!

Secondly, Dickens was a fierce critic of the New Poor Law and the workhouse system. Oliver Twist was serialised in the late 1830s and contained vivid descriptions of the horrors of workhouse life. Throughout his career his invective against the effects of the New Poor Law continued. In the last novel he completed, *Our Mutual Friend*, the character Betty Higden was asked why she reacted so strongly to the mention of the poor house:

> 'Dislike the mention of it?' answered the old woman. 'Kill me sooner
> than take me there. Throw this child under cart-horses' feet and a
> loaded wagon, sooner than take him there. Come to us and find us all
> a-dying, and set a light to us all where we lie, and let us all blaze away
> 5 with the house into a heap of cinders, sooner than move a corpse of us
> there!

Though Dickens' hostility to the Poor Law failed to bring about its repeal in his own lifetime, it did contribute to a growing unease at the way the poor were treated by authority.

3 The Changing Background to the Debate

> **KEY ISSUE** In what ways did political, social and economic changes
> in the second half of the nineteenth century lead to changing atti-
> tudes towards poverty?

Three developments in the second half of the nineteenth century underpinned the changing debate on the treatment of poverty: firstly, the growth of the electorate; secondly, the spread of state interven-tion; thirdly, the relative decline of the British economy.

The Great Reform Act of 1832 had extended the right to vote to most middle-class men. However, in the first half of the century the working classes were excluded from direct participation in national electoral politics. Leading figures were opposed to any extension of the franchise which they believed would result in disaster. 'Power in the hands of the masses,' according to Lord Palmerston, 'throws the scum of the community to the surface.' Yet, in the last third of the century, this stance began to change as the ruling classes felt it neces-sary to enfranchise increasing numbers of working-class men. The 1867 Reform Act gave the right to vote to an extra one million men, including skilled artisans. A further act of 1884 resulted in 6 out of 10 men having the vote. The major political parties now faced a situation where they had to appeal to working men if they wanted to get their votes, and social welfare legislation was perceived as a way to do this. More importantly, the spectre of socialism and social revolution in Europe and the appearance of revolutionary parties like the Social Democratic Federation (SDF) in Britain, convinced some politicians that welfare reform was essential in order to tempt the working class away from more radical politics. In an 1895 speech A.J. Balfour, soon to be a Conservative Prime Minister, argued that collective action through social legislation was the 'most effective antidote' to socialism.

The spread of state intervention pre-dated the late nineteenth-century concerns about the dangers of socialism. Despite theoretical support for the idea of *laissez-faire*, governments from the 1860s onwards were increasingly prepared to take action to ameliorate social problems. Factory and workshop legislation limited the rights of industrialists to over-work their employees and forced them to provide basic minimum standards of safety. Public Health Acts, most famously that of 1875, forced local authorities to overcome the objections of property owners and provide water and sanitation in their areas. The 1870 Education Act established state education and was followed in 1880 by legislation which made elementary school attendance compulsory. A consensus had developed that it was not tolerable for workers to be mangled by unguarded machines, for sewage to run down the streets or for children to grow up without a minimum education. As the State accepted responsibility for these elements of social life so, it was argued, it should take some responsibility for the problem of poverty.

The 1880s and 1890s also witnessed a growing concern about Britain's position in the world. The 1851 Great Exhibition allowed most Victorians to celebrate the high point of British industrial supremacy. But the complacency of the mid-Victorian period was shaken by the realisation that other nations, such as Germany and the USA, were challenging British economic power. Historians disagree as to the severity of the 'Great Depression' of 1873-96, but at the time people certainly believed that something had gone wrong.[1] The very terms 'unemployed' and 'unemployment' entered the currency of debate in the 1880s. Unemployment figures for this period are unreliable, but as many as 10 per cent of workers were out of work in 1886. In 1895 a House of Commons Select Committee on Distress from Want of Employment was established, the first enquiry of its kind and an indication of the concern of the authorities. Charles Darwin's ideas about evolution and the survival of the fittest were also under intense discussion at this time and some commentators argued that the impoverished condition of the British race was the reason for Britain's apparent failure in the battle for economic survival. Politicians began to suggest that economic decline was a consequence of decline in the efficiency of the population. This 'national efficiency' debate gathered momentum at the turn of the century and encouraged some politicians to believe that state sponsored social welfare was essential in order to protect Britain's position in the world. The dramatic revelations about the extent of poverty which were published at the time added considerable fuel to the fire of this debate.

4 The Growing Awareness of Poverty in the Late Nineteenth Century

> **KEY ISSUE** What new ideas about the causes of, and solutions to, the problem of poverty were suggested by the investigations of Charles Booth and Seebohm Rowntree?

a) Charles Booth

Charles Booth was born in 1840 into a wealthy Liverpool trading family. He inherited £20,000 on the death of his father and, with his brother, Alfred, set up a business which expanded into a large and prosperous steamship company. Though plagued by poor health, Booth was a prodigiously hard worker. He was an earnest man, anxious to do good in the world as well as make money. In the mid 1870s, after a spell in Switzerland recovering from serious ill-health, Booth, his wife Mary and their two children settled in London. Here they quickly became involved with the debates regarding poverty and philanthropy, particularly as Mary Booth's uncle was a leading light in the Charity Organisation Society and her cousins worked with the philanthropic housing reformer and leading COS figure, Octavia Hill.

Booth did not agree with the COS notion that the poor were entirely responsible for their own condition. On the other hand, he rejected the socialist argument that the capitalist system itself was the cause of poverty. After some involvement with the Mansion House Enquiry into Unemployment of 1885, the following year Booth decided to investigate the realities of poverty for himself. Working with a small team, he estimated that the project would last three years. Seventeen years and seventeen volumes later, *Life and Labour in the People of London* was finally completed.

Booth and his team attempted to classify the population according to the nature of their work, earnings and style of life. He acknowledged that the classes he identified shaded into one another and overlapped at the fringes, but he believed that the distinctions between these classes were fundamental to the understanding of poverty and prosperity. At the bottom of the social scale were class A, described as the lowest class of occasional labourers, loafers and semi-criminals. Booth believed this to be a largely 'hereditary' class: people were born into class A and were rarely able to escape from it. The lives of those in class A were characterised by disorder. Booth wrote that, 'they degrade whatever they touch', and he variously described them as 'savages' and 'barbarians'. Fortunately, Booth found that only 0.9 per cent of the population were in class A.

Above the lowest group were class B, characterised by casual earnings. Because their work was low-paid and sporadic, the 7.5 per cent of the population in this class were 'very poor'. Casual dock workers were the largest occupation within class B. Booth believed that these people were, for 'mental, moral or physical reasons', incapable of better work. Class C had better earnings than B but their work was irregular and their income intermittent. They might earn 15s. to 20s. a week when they were employed, but they were involved in a constant struggle to make ends meet. Class D also had low incomes (not more than 21s. per week) but at least they had regular work. They tended to be more prudent than those in class C but, like them, were 'poor'. C and D together made up 22.3 per cent of the population.

Classes E and F were in 'comfort' rather than poverty. Together, they comprised 51.5 per cent of the population. Class E were workers in regular employment earning 22s. to 30s. per week. Class F were the best paid artisans and workmen. Classes G and H were the lower and upper middle classes and constituted 17.8 per cent of the population.

With such an enormous survey (to which must be added various other texts and the investigators' surviving research notes), it is little wonder that historians have disagreed as to Booth's message. Nevertheless, two key findings regarding poverty seem to have emerged from this gigantic study. Firstly, Booth's calculations demonstrated that 30.7 per cent of the London population were living in poverty. This was a shocking statistic and one which was taken up by social reformers as an indication of the scale of the problem. Secondly, Booth showed that poverty was a consequence of circumstance as much as individual folly. In a sample of 4000 'poor' (classes C and D) and 'very poor' (classes A and B) households, Booth attempted to quantify the causes of poverty (see the bar chart below).

These figures indicated that most poverty was caused by problems

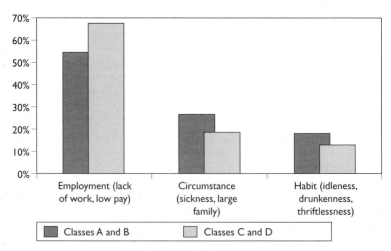

Reasons for Poverty

relating to employment. In particular, Booth drew attention to the problem of irregularity of work. Many of the poor people in classes B and C found that work was only available for a few days in the week or at certain times of the year. This meant that it was impossible for them to organise their lives with any certainty because they did not know what their income would be, in some cases from one day to the next. Booth did not abandon the idea of individual responsibility: he used subjective terms like 'shiftless' to describe some groups. However, he emphasised that poverty was still poverty whatever the cause. He pointed out that it was easy for the comfortable middle classes to criticise the poor for their behaviour, but that it was not so easy for anyone to lead a regular life when faced with such irregularity of income. Unlike many contemporary social commentators, Booth did not condemn the working classes for drinking, and saw drink as a consequence of poverty as much as a cause of it.

Despite the monumental achievements of Booth's study, *Life and Labour of the People in London* was criticised at the time. Helen Bosanquet of the COS attacked the statistical basis of the investigation which she claimed underestimated the sources of income available to poor families. This criticism suggested that Booth overestimated the extent of poverty. Bosanquet maintained that only the individual case-work of the COS could reveal the true circumstances of the poor. Although Booth's investigators had spent some time living in poor neighbourhoods, most of their work was based on the evidence of school board visitors and other middle-class groups who came into contact with the poor. It has also been pointed out that his definition of 'the line of poverty' was imprecise and varied throughout the study.

Historians have also found fault with the accuracy of Booth's work, though not necessarily from the same perspective. The historian Karel Williams noted that, as part of the investigation, Booth surveyed school teachers as to their opinion of how many children were in poverty. This survey suggested that 45 per cent of the population was in poverty - a much higher figure than the 30.7 per cent indicated by the school board visitors. Williams and others have also criticised Booth's failure to come up with convincing solutions to the problems he discovered: he never abandoned his individualist views despite his discovery of the extent of the problem.[2]

In one area Booth did suggest a radical form of action by the State. He believed that the group identified as class B were 'The crux of the problem'. Class A, though the most degraded, were small in number and could be dealt with through a mixture of charity and tough policing. Class B were both more numerous and more problematic. This group dragged classes C and D into poverty by their inadequacy and their inability to maintain themselves at a decent standard. Class B's lack of ability, added to the hazards of casualised work, meant that it was impossible for its members to help themselves. The only solution was to remove them from the labour market altogether by placing them in state run labour colonies: a form of 'state slavery' as Booth himself admitted. The removal of class B from the labour market would provide more employment opportunities for classes C and D and allow them to rise out of poverty. Such a proposal demonstrated both a ruthless determination to deal with poverty and a ruthless disregard for the individual rights of some of the poor. But the fact that even a confirmed individualist like Charles Booth could come up with such a collectivist solution, even if it was a harsh one, is an indication that attitudes towards poverty were shifting.

Booth also believed in a collectivist solution to the issue of poverty amongst the elderly. In 1894 he published a survey entitled *The Aged Poor in England and Wales* in which he claimed that 40-45 per cent of the elderly were living in poverty. In 1893 he had been recruited onto the Royal Commission on the Aged Poor. Here he was an advocate of old age pensions which he believed should be provided by the State, without the need for the elderly themselves to have paid into any pension scheme. The proposal was rejected on the grounds that it would cost too much, but Booth had forced a radical solution onto the agenda.

By revealing that 30.7 per cent of the population of London were in poverty, by indicating that poverty was caused by economic circumstance more than individual failure, and by suggesting that the State had to take a bigger role in dealing with this problem, Charles Booth had a profound impact on the debate about poverty and welfare.

b) Seebohm Rowntree

Seebohm Rowntree was a member of the famous York chocolate and cocoa producing family. As devout Quakers, the Rowntrees had shown a philanthropic concern for the welfare of their workers and Seebohm was, like Booth, interested in gaining more precise information on the lives and conditions of labouring people. One of the criticisms of Booth's *Life and Labour of the People in London* was that its findings were unrepresentative. The metropolis inevitably attracted the poor from elsewhere, drawn by the bright lights and the chance of work. Was the 30.7 per cent of Londoners living in poverty really typical of the rest of the country? Rowntree hoped to build on Booth's work by conducting a similar investigation into his own city, York. He also hoped to give more precision to Booth's idea of a line of income below which poverty could be said to exist.

Rowntree published *Poverty: A Study of Town Life* in 1901. The investigation consisted of three distinct elements. Firstly, Rowntree's investigator visited the homes of the wage earners of York. About two-thirds of the population were visited and the information gained was supplemented by reports from other sources such as the local clergy. On the basis of this data, a decision was made as to whether or not households appeared to be 'in obvious want or squalor'. This total turned out to be some 28 per cent of the population. Secondly, Rowntree obtained information on the incomes of wage earners from local employers. Thirdly, he calculated the minimum income necessary for a family to exist at 'mere physical efficiency'. This sum was 21s 8d. for a family of five. Rowntree stressed that this 'poverty line' was the absolute minimum:

1   Let us clearly understand what 'merely physical efficiency' means. A family living upon the scale allowed for in this estimate must never spend a penny on railway fare or omnibus. They must never go into the country unless they walk. They must never purchase a halfpenny news-
5   paper or spend a penny to buy a ticket for a popular concert. They must write no letters to absent children, for they cannot afford to pay the postage. They must never contribute to their church or chapel, or give any help to a neighbour which costs them money. They cannot save, nor can they join sick club or Trade Union, because they cannot
10 pay the necessary subscriptions. The children must have no pocket money for dolls, marbles, or sweets. The father must smoke no tobacco, and must drink no beer. The mother must never buy any pretty clothes for herself or for her children, the character of the family wardrobe as for the family diet, being governed by the regulation, 'nothing must be
15 bought but that which is absolutely necessary for the maintenance of physical health, and what is bought must be of the plainest and most economical description.' Should a child fall ill, it must be attended by the parish doctor; should it die, it must be buried by the parish. Finally, the wage-earner must never be absent from his work for a
20 single day.

On this basis, matching incomes to minimum expenditure, Rowntree demonstrated that just under 10 per cent of the population of York

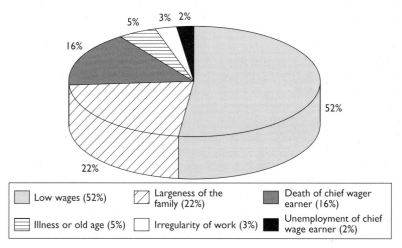

Reasons for primary poverty in York, 1899

were living, somehow, beneath the poverty line. Their incomes were insufficient to meet the minimum outgoings needed to survive. This type of distress Rowntree called 'primary poverty'. He also investigated the reasons for this primary poverty and concluded that in most cases low wages were the cause.

Rowntree concentrated on the 10 per cent of the population living below the line of 'merely physical efficiency'. But despite the way in which he defined this as the 'poverty line', these were not the only poor in York. His investigator had found 28 per cent of those visited were in poverty. By subtracting the 10 per cent in primary poverty from the initial 28 per cent found to be 'in obvious want or squalor', Rowntree calculated that the remaining 18 per cent were in 'secondary poverty'. He defined this group as,

> Families whose total earnings would be sufficient for the maintenance of merely physical efficiency were it not that some portion of it is absorbed by other expenditure, either useful or wasteful.

Though Rowntree did blame alcohol for some of this 'other expenditure', he accepted that people had legitimate social and recreational needs which they were entitled to satisfy. It was unreasonable to expect people always to spend their money only on the absolute essentials.

Rowntree went on to develop the idea of life-cycle poverty. This showed that the degree of poverty experienced by families changed over time. Typically, a young couple might be relatively prosperous when first married, especially if they were both earning. As they had children, their prosperity would decline with the possible loss of the mother's income and the cost of feeding and clothing the children. At this point, many families might slip below the poverty line. As the children reached working age the family income would again rise for a period. But when the children left home and old age deprived the parents of their earning power, poverty might return once more. At any of these stages illness, the death of a wage earner or the loss of regular work could also plunge the family deeper below the poverty line.

Just as she had attacked the work of Charles Booth, so Helen Bosanquet of the COS also criticised Rowntree.[3] Again, she claimed that he had overestimated the proportion of those in poverty by setting the poverty line at too high a level. This was somewhat ironic as Rowntree had set the line at a deliberately low level precisely to counter this type of criticism. Indeed, later in his life he made the point that the level of austerity represented by 21 shillings and 8 pence allowed basic physical survival but was not adequate to meet people's essential social and psychological needs:

> ... working people are just as human as those with more money. They cannot live on a 'fodder' basis. They crave for relaxation and recreation just as the rest of us do. But ... they can only get these things by going short of something which is essential to physical fitness, and so they go short ...

Rowntree's poverty line only measured those who were in primary poverty. The two-thirds of the poor who were above the line were still poor, even if they had a little bit more than the bare necessities essential for physical survival.

Rowntree's work, as with that of Booth, had a major impact on the understanding of poverty at the turn of the century. His finding that 28 per cent of the population of York were living in poverty was close to Booth's conclusion that 31 per cent of the London population were poor. This suggested that poverty on this scale was a national rather than just a London problem. Rowntree's precise identification of the primary poverty line made an important contribution to the debate about the causes of poverty. At a time when the belief that poverty was caused by wasteful and extravagant spending was still very strong, Rowntree showed that, no matter how thrifty they were, the 10 per cent of the population in primary poverty simply had insufficient to live on. He also demonstrated that the causes of this poverty were circumstances, such as low wages, that were beyond the control of the individual. Rowntree drew on his scientific background as a research chemist and his use of statistics gave his work an apparent scientific precision that lent authority to his views. Finally, Rowntree's enumeration of the causes of primary poverty and his development of the idea of life cycle poverty gave direction to the search for welfare solutions to the problem of poverty. If unemployment, children, illness and old age were key causes, the State could target its support for the poor into these areas. Rowntree was a political activist as well as a social researcher, and these conclusions were to prove influential in the formation of Liberal Party welfare policy at the beginning of the twentieth century.

References

1   S.B. Saul, *The Myth of the Great Depression* (Macmillan, 1969).
2   Karel Williams, *From Pauperism to Poverty* (Routledge & Kegan Paul, 1981), p. 323.
3   Jane Lewis, *Social facts, social theory and social change*, in David Englander and Rosemary O'Day (eds), *Retrieved Riches: Social Investigation in Britain 1840-1914* (Scolar Press, 1995), p. 58.

This chapter is mainly about attitudes and how they changed. The best way to make notes is to concentrate on the writers mentioned in the chapter. You will need to summarise the new contributions they made to the understanding of poverty and the poor.

Summary Diagram
Changing Attitudes to Poverty 1850-1900

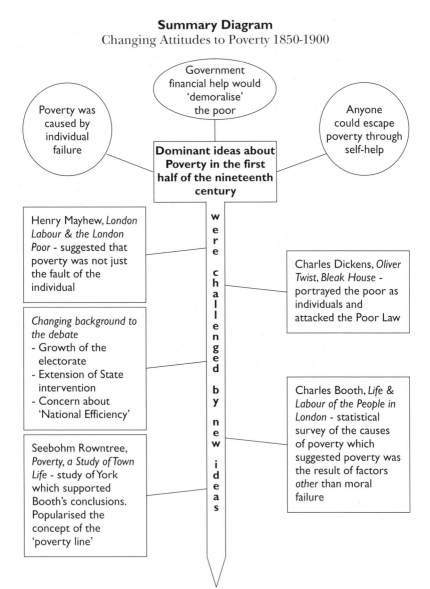

Source-based questions on Chapter 5

1. Describing the poor

Read the extracts from Henry Mayhew and Charles Dickens (pages 82, 83, 84 and 85)

a) What were the reasons for the poverty of the ham sandwich seller described by Henry Mayhew on page 82? (2 marks)
b) How does the language and tone of the extract from *Bleak House* indicate Dickens' sympathy with the plight of the poor? (4 marks)
c) To what extent are the extracts from Mayhew more reliable than the extracts from Dickens as sources for the historian studying poverty in this period? (6 marks)

2. Researching poverty

Look at the graphs based on the research of Booth and Rowntree (pages 88 and 91).

a) In what ways did the research of Booth and Rowntree challenge contemporary views as to the causes of poverty? (4 marks)
b) Is the information in the bar chart based on Booth's work supported by the information in the pie chart based on Rowntree's work? Explain your answer. (6 marks)
c) How reliable are statistics, such as these graphs, as sources of information about poverty in the late nineteenth and early twentieth centuries? (6 marks)

3. The Poverty Line

Read the extract from Seebohm Rowntree on page 91.
a) According to Rowntree, what were the consequences of living on 21s 8d per week? (3 marks)
b) What aspects of Rowntree's description might have been particularly shocking to a middle-class reader? (3 marks)
c) What criticisms could be made of Rowntree's 'poverty line'? (3 marks)

6 The Liberal Social Reforms 1906-14

POINTS TO CONSIDER

This chapter examines the important welfare measures passed by the Liberal government immediately before the First World War. In order to understand the motives behind these initiatives it is important for you to understand the reasons why the Liberals embarked on such a radical programme. The Poor Law Commission of 1905-09 provides an important context for the reforms. The social reforms themselves dealt with the welfare of children, the elderly, the low paid, the unemployed and the sick. You need to examine what each measure did and determine how far it represented a new departure in the treatment of poverty.

KEY DATES

1900   Formation of the Labour Representation Committee. Beginning of Labour Party.

1903   Joseph Chamberlain announces support for Protectionism. Conservative party splits on this issue.

1904   Report of the Inter-Departmental Committee on Physical Deterioration. Revealed poor condition of many school-children.

1905   Unemployed Workmen Act. Local authorities set up Distress Committees to provide work for the unemployed.

1905   December: Liberals form a minority government following the resignation of Conservative Prime Minister Balfour. Liberals immediately call a General Election.

1906   January: Liberals win General Election with landslide majority.

1906   Education (Provision of Meals) Act. Free school meals for poor children.

1907   Education (Administrative Provisions) Act. Medical inspections for school children.

1908   Children Act. Reformed the law relating to children.

1905-09   Royal Commission on the Poor Laws. Criticised the current operation of the Poor Law, but members divided on how to reform it.

1908   Old Age Pensions Act. First state pensions. Given to those over 70.

1909   Trade Boards Act. Minimum wages established in certain low-paid industries.

1909   Labour Exchanges Act. Offices set up to advise the unemployed of vacancies.

1911   National Insurance Act. Compulsory health and unemployment insurance.

Apart from a short-lived administration in the 1890s, the Liberals had been out of office for 20 years before they came into office in December 1905 and won the 1906 General Election with a landslide majority. Welfare reform was not the main issue on which they had fought the election, yet within a decade the Liberals had passed a set of measures which radically changed the way government dealt with the issue of poverty. There is no simple explanation of why the Liberals embarked on this period of social reform, but at least five factors need to be examined in order to understand their motivation. The aims of the Liberals in passing this legislation clearly had a major influence on the nature of the legislation. Were they consciously attempting to make a radical break with the past, or were they just responding to pressing problems in a pragmatic, practical fashion?

1 Reasons for the Liberal Social Reforms

> **KEY ISSUE** Were the Liberal reforms motivated by genuine concerns about poverty, or were they a result of other political and economic pressures?

a) The Liberal Election Success

If the Liberals had failed to win the 1906 General Election they would not have been in a position to introduce any social reforms. The Conservatives had dominated politics in the late nineteenth century and had won the 1900 General Election with a big majority, so Liberal success in 1906 was far from inevitable. A continuation of Conservative government would have been highly unlikely to produce such a burst of reform. They had passed the 1905 Unemployed Workmen Act, which established distress committees in all major towns and cities; these had the authority to provide temporary relief works for the unemployed. However, this was a short-term response to an immediate crisis, and the Conservatives had shown little inclination to deal with other aspects of poverty.

Historians are in general agreement that the Liberals did not win the 1906 General Election because they promised social reform.[1] Henry Campbell-Bannerman, the Liberal leader, was reluctant to commit his party to action on old age pensions or unemployment, and nearly a third of Liberal candidates failed to mention Poor Law reform or pensions in their election addresses. The dominant themes of the campaign were in fact Free Trade and 'Chinese Slavery'.

Free Trade had become an issue because of leading Unionist Joseph Chamberlain's decision to support a policy of protectionism in 1903. Protectionism meant the establishment of customs duties and tariffs to protect British goods from cheap foreign imports. As the price of foreign goods rose because of these tariffs, it was believed that people would buy the relatively cheaper home produced items. This would lead to a drop in unemployment as the increase in demand forced employers to take on more labour. Chamberlain, who had implemented a major programme of housing and health reforms as Mayor of Birmingham in the 1880s, also believed that the revenue generated by tariff reform could be used to finance welfare reforms such as old age pensions. However, Free Trade was the policy traditionally associated with Britain's industrial prosperity and had been elevated to a moral principle by Liberals in the mid-Victorian era. Chamberlain's initiative divided the Conservatives between protectionists, free-traders and moderates who wanted a compromise. On the other hand, it united the hitherto divided Liberals: 98 per cent of their candidates mentioned the defence of Free Trade in their election addresses. Crucially, the Liberals successfully portrayed the threatened introduction of tariffs on imported grain as a 'bread tax' which would force up the price of food. This was electorally disastrous for the Conservatives.

'Chinese Slavery' was the title given to the practice of shipping Chinese labourers into Britain's South African territories as cheap labour. The appalling conditions and lack of freedom to which these workers were subjected became a scandal, and the Conservative government's failure to take action cost them votes. Liberal and particularly Labour candidates were quick to link this with the Conservatives' failure to overturn the Taff Vale judgement of 1901. This legal case had, in effect, prevented trade unions from going on strike, and trade unionists claimed that it was part of a process designed to worsen workers' conditions in Britain as well as in the empire.

The issues of free trade and Chinese workers did great damage to the Conservatives. Other factors also contributed to their defeat. Improved Liberal organisation meant that a much higher proportion of seats were contested and the higher turn out in 1906 compared to 1900 helped the Liberal and Labour votes. The newly formed Labour Party entered into an electoral pact with the Liberals: the parties agreed not to not stand against each other and this prevented the anti-Conservative vote being split. The final result, which saw the Conservatives reduced to 157 seats and the Liberals increased to 400, was the product of a wide range of policies and circumstances. However, the social reform issue played a very small part in causing the Liberals' victory.

b) The Threat of Socialism

The Liberal social reforms can be seen as a response to the perceived growth of socialism at the start of the twentieth century. In 1899 the Trade Union Congress (TUC) decided that organised labour needed a political voice. The following year they set up the Labour Representation Committee (LRC) and in 1906 this became the Labour Party. The immediate goal of Labour representatives was to secure the legal position of the trade unions, but both the TUC and the Labour Party were also committed to a programme of social reforms, including the abolition of the Poor Laws and the introduction of benefits such as old age pensions. Twenty-nine Labour MPs were elected in 1906 and, although they supported the new government, many Liberals felt that Labour had the potential to replace them as the main alternative to the Conservatives. By introducing their own programme of social reform some Liberals believed that they could out-trump Labour and stop the working-class vote defecting to them.

At a deeper level, politicians in both the Liberal and Conservative parties were worried about the potential threat of socialism. The Labour Party had committed itself to a moderate and non-revolutionary programme, but there was a concern that a much more radical brand of socialism, committed to the destruction of the capitalist system, might arise if action was not taken to improve conditions for the working classes. Germany was seen as a good example of a state where the government, especially under Chancellor Bismarck between 1871 and 1890, had limited the growth of socialism by the introduction of social reforms. David Lloyd George, the Liberal Chancellor of the Exchequer, went on a visit to Germany in 1908 to investigate their welfare system. Winston Churchill, the President of the Board of Trade, wrote to Prime Minister Herbert Asquith in the same year recommending that the government:

> thrust a big slice of Bismarckianism over the whole underside of our industrial system, and await the consequences whatever they may be with a good conscience.

Churchill and Lloyd George both represented a more radical strand of Liberalism which was a key influence on the shape of the Liberal reforms.

c) New Liberalism

'New Liberalism' emerged in the 1890s as a radical tendency within the Liberal Party. Whereas traditional 'Gladstonian' Liberalism had believed in low taxation and a minimal, *laissez-faire* role for the State, New Liberalism stood for increased taxes on the rich in order to finance state intervention on behalf of the poor. Intellectually underpinned by the writings of the Oxford philosopher T.H. Green, and popularised by newspapers such as the *Manchester Guardian, Daily Chronicle* and *Daily News,* New Liberalism was given a powerful impetus by the revelations of Booth and Rowntree (see pages 87-93). Many New Liberals were involved with the settlement movement. This was a scheme whereby university graduates would spend some time living in poor areas, working on education and other projects. The most famous of these, Toynbee Hall in East London, was also a base for Booth's researches. Confronted with the realities of poverty, New Liberals realised that old Liberal beliefs had to be amended in the light of persistent poverty. Liberal MP J.M. Robertson explained that,

> *Laissez-faire* is not done with as a principle of rational limitation of state interference, but it is quite done with as a pretext for leaving uncured deadly social evils which admit of curative treatment by state action.

New Liberalism gradually became the dominant force in Liberal politics at the beginning of the twentieth century. Its key supporters, J.A. Hobson, L.T. Hobhouse and Herbert Samuel, were all talented writers as well as politicians and by 1906 many in the party had come to accept New Liberal ideas. In the Liberal Government, Churchill and Lloyd George were the most prominent New Liberals but H.H. Asquith, who was Chancellor of the Exchequer from 1906 to 1908 and then Prime Minister, also accepted the need for redistributive taxation and welfare reforms.

d) Unemployment

While the investigations of Booth and Rowntree had shown that the poorest sections of the population were in a more or less permanent state of distress, the late nineteenth and early twentieth centuries also saw a growing awareness of a different cause of poverty. Unemployment could be a problem not just for the 'residuum' of casualised and marginal workers, but could also plunge even skilled and 'respectable' workers into poverty. In the mid-Victorian period there had been an assumption that economic growth would lead to an increasing demand for labour, but the 'Great Depression' of 1873-96 and the growth of foreign competition forced a reassessment. It became clear that periodic spells of mass unemployment were possibly inevitable as the pattern of trade went from boom to slump. The Poor Law was not designed to deal with this type of crisis: the forces causing distress had nothing to do with the failure of the individual and workhouses simply could not accommodate the numbers involved. In 1886 a meeting of 20,000 unemployed workers in Trafalgar Square had developed into a riot. Following this, the government had encouraged Poor Law guardians to establish temporary work schemes to alleviate distress (see pages 50-51). The 1905 Unemployed Workmen Act was also passed following an

A work scheme for the unemployed: Poplar, London, 1905

increase in unemployment and demonstrations. Again, this Act allowed local Distress Committees to establish relief work for the unemployed.

The Liberals in opposition had to demonstrate that they were also concerned and, despite the reservations of their leader, Henry Campbell Bannerman, it was clear that once in government they would be forced to take action. Liberal Chief Whip, Herbert Gladstone, outlined his party's thinking in 1905:

1 Genuine workmen in thousands are demoralised by being forced to depend upon this private charity or the workhouse. I don't suggest that the Government should bear the whole burden. But the action of Municipal and other public bodies should be organised and co-
5 ordinated, and where the burden is too great for local action, other opportunities for temporary employment ought to be provided by Government which would not tempt men from their ordinary trades but would give them a wage sufficient for the support of themselves and their families, and which would be profitable to the
10 state.

Though lacking in detail, the Liberals had committed themselves to some degree of intervention on behalf of the unemployed.

e) National Efficiency

Towards the end of the nineteenth century, concerns were increasingly expressed regarding the 'efficiency' of the British population. The success of foreign economies suggested that the British workforce was inferior to that of the foreign rivals the Nation faced. The work of Booth and Rowntree, by revealing the depths of poverty in English cities, reinforced this concern. What really alarmed some people was the prospect of this 'national deterioration' weakening Britain's military capability, and the Boer War of 1899-1902 seemed to confirm the worst of these fears. Not only had British forces struggled to overcome an inferior enemy, but the details that emerged from army recruiting centres suggested that a high proportion of volunteers had been rejected on the grounds of physical incapacity. In his 1901 book *Efficiency and Empire* Arnold White reported that, 'two out of three men willing to bear arms in the Manchester district are virtually invalids', and in 1903 Major-General Sir Frederick Maurice claimed that only two out of five enlisted men remained fit for service after two years. This, he stressed, was not a reflection on the hardships of army life but on the level of unfitness within the population.

The result of these concerns was the appointment, in 1903, of a Government Inter-Departmental Committee to enquire into the extent of the problem. The Committee found that there was no evidence that the British 'race' was deteriorating in the way that some had claimed, but it did confirm that the physical condition of the poorest parts of the population was a cause for concern:

1 With regard to physical degeneracy, the children frequenting the poorer schools of London and the large towns betray a most serious condition of affairs, calling for ameliorative and arrestive measures, the most important features being the apathy of parents as regards the school, the lack
5 of parental care of children, the poor physique, powers of endurance, and educational attainments of the children attending school.

If parents were failing to exercise proper care over the welfare of their children, then the State would have to undertake the responsibility for providing the welfare necessary. Such a conclusion clearly provided at least part of an agenda for a future government interested in social reform.

2 The Royal Commission on the Poor Laws, 1905-09

> **KEY ISSUE** What principles for welfare reform were suggested by the two reports of the 1905-1909 Royal Commission on the Poor Laws?

In 1904 the Conservative government decided to establish a Royal Commission to enquire into the working of the Poor Laws and the relief of distress. The immediate cause was the growing problem of unemployment, but there were also increasing concerns about the suitability of the Poor Law as a means of dealing with poverty in the new century. The Commission, which met the following year, was chaired by Lord George Hamilton, and its 20 members shared a wide range of expertise on the subject: they included Poor law guardians, civil servants from the Local Government Board, leading members of the Charity Organisation Society, religious leaders, trade unionists and the social investigators Charles Booth and Beatrice Webb. The detailed inquiry conducted by the Commission ran to 47 volumes and was the result of hundreds of interviews and visits. Though much of the evidence did point to the inadequacies of the workhouse system, the Local Government Board seemed determined to return to the principles of 1834. When questioned by the Commission, J.S. Davy, the civil servant in charge of the Poor Law Division, confirmed that the loss of personal reputation, personal freedom (through detention in the workhouse) and political rights should continue to form the main elements of ineligibility.

The commissioners themselves were divided over what should be done to reform the system and two reports were produced. The Majority Report, inspired by Helen Bosanquet and the COS members, accepted the need for a reform of the system. It criticised the working of the Boards of Guardians and the indiscriminate and excessive use of outdoor relief, but it also acknowledged 'the unsuitability of the general workhouse as a test or deterrent for the able-bodied'. COS influence was especially clear in the judgement that, 'the causes of distress are not only economic and industrial; in their origin and character they are largely moral', and in the complaints about the lack of co-operation between the Poor Law and charities. The Majority Report recommended the replacement of the Boards of Guardians by Public Assistance Committees. These would be made up of elected local councillors and local philanthropists. Individual case-work was encouraged as the key strategy for dealing with poverty and Voluntary Aid Committees, representing local charities, would be established to facilitate this.

The Majority Report accepted that the Poor Law should continue to be the main institution dealing with poverty. This was unacceptable to some of the Commissioners, who believed that much more fundamental reform was required. They produced a Minority Report which was inspired by commissioner Beatrice Webb and her husband Sydney. The Webbs were socialists and leading members of the Fabian Society, one of the founding organisations of the new Labour Party. The Minority Report was signed by Mrs Webb herself, the socialist Guardian George Lansbury, the trade unionist Francis Chandler and the Dean of Norwich, Russell Wakefield. It emphasised the economic cause of poverty and the need for the State to take action to deal with unemployment. The Minority Report also recommended the break up of the Poor Law. Its authors recommended that specialist committees should be set up by local councils to deal with specific types of poverty: education committees to deal with issues of child poverty; health committees to deal with the sick and disabled; pensions committees to deal with the elderly poor. They believed that the problem of unemployment was beyond the capacity of local authorities and recommended the establishment of a government Ministry of Labour to deal with this issue. Massive public work schemes, a national system of labour exchanges to help the unemployed find work, training schemes and maintenance payments for those who remained out of work would constitute a comprehensive programme to be provided by this ministry.

The split within the Commission was an important reason why neither report resulted in direct government action. The recommendations of the majority seemed inadequate to the New Liberals, while the enthusiastic campaigning of the Webbs seems to have alienated the government. Nevertheless, the work of the Commission kept the issues of poverty, unemployment and welfare at the forefront of public debate. This in itself strongly encouraged the Liberals to come up with solutions to these problems. Indeed, the government had already begun to take action before the Commission reported in 1909.

3 The Liberal Social Reforms

> **KEY ISSUE** To what extent did each of the Liberal social reforms mark a significant break with nineteenth-century attitudes to poverty and the poor?

Each of the Liberal welfare measures had its roots in particular concerns and circumstances as well as in a general desire to reform the way government tackled poverty. The Liberals did not come to power with a coherent programme of reform, and they were not working to a pre-determined plan. However, the reforms did address all the key areas of poverty identified in the reports and investigations of the previous decade, and it is useful to examine them with these areas in mind: poverty in childhood; poverty in old age; and poverty due to low pay; unemployment and ill health.

a) Poverty in Childhood

The report of the Inter-Departmental Committee on Physical Deterioration of 1904 had drawn particular attention to poverty in childhood as a source of unfitness in adults. The Liberal government's first pieces of social legislation were a response to this concern, although the link was not a direct one. In many ways, the legislation on children illustrates that change came as a result of pressure from a wide range of other groups, rather than just depending on the commitment of the Liberals.

The Education (Provision of Meals) Act of 1906 allowed local authorities to provide school meals for children who were in need. The Liberals had shown no urgency in this area, but the introduction of a private member's bill by the Labour MP, William Wilson, forced them to make their minds up. The government decided to adopt the measure. There was a major issue at stake because the opponents of free school meals argued that they undermined the role of the parent. Writing in 1906 Sir Arthur Clay warned that,

1   to feed a child is to give relief to its parents, and the effect must be to undermine their independence and self-reliance, and to give to their children an object-lesson in the evasion of responsibility which will never be forgotten, and which will bear fruit when they in turn become
5   parents.

Not surprisingly the COS supported this position, with Helen Bosanquet maintaining that free school meals would have the effect of 'permanently demoralising large numbers of the population' and would lead to the break-up of the family as parents lost the incentive to provide for their offspring.

The 1906 Act set one precedent by overcoming these objections and allowing the State to take responsibility for something previously considered a family responsibility. It set another by not disenfranchising the parents of the children concerned. An important element in the stigmatisation of those claiming Poor Law relief had been the withdrawal of the claimant's right to vote, if he had one in the first place (women at this time had no right to vote in national elections, although they did have the vote in local politics). This was based on the notion that those who 'took' from the State, rather than contributed to it, were somehow less than full citizens. The government had now accepted that those in need who received benefits were entitled to retain their full rights as citizens.

If the immediate pressure for free school meals had come from the emerging Labour Party, the inspiration for school medical inspections came from within the Government's own civil service. Professor Oliver MacDonagh has argued that a central reason for the growth of state intervention was pressure from the professional bureaucracy employed by the State which was always concerned to expand its own influence.[2] This could be for reasons of empire building or arising from a genuine desire to make things better. The Education (Administrative Provisions) Act of 1907 is good evidence to support McDonagh's theory. Sir Robert Morant, Permanent Secretary at the Board of Education, was unimpressed by the radicalism of his political masters and decided that he would make things happen despite them. He buried the recommendations for school medical inspections in clause 13 of a complicated piece of legislation and MPs failed to pick up the significance of the measure when it was debated in Parliament. Once passed, Morant followed up the Act by issuing two administrative circulars to Local Education Authorities regulating the operation of inspections and authorising them to provide medical treatment, as well as inspection.

Like the 1906 School Meals Act, the 1907 Act was not something that the Liberal government had planned. And also like the 1906 Act, the principle was contentious. State interference in the medical welfare of children was said to undermine the role of parents, in the same way that school meals were said to have a similar effect. Yet both measures gradually had a major impact despite their opponents. Although the 1906 Act was at first permissive (Local Education Authorities were not compelled to supply school meals), by 1914 over 14 million meals per annum were being provided for 158,000 children. In a similar way, the 1907 Act did not compel local authorities to set up clinics, but by 1914 most were providing some medical treatment for children.

The 1908 Children Act was a deliberate reform by the Liberal Government, although it too was heavily influenced by the lobbying of pressure groups like the National Society for the Prevention of Cruelty to Children. The Act brought together dozens of older pieces of legislation and added new measures. Penalties were imposed on parents who abused or neglected their children and the Poor Law authorities were made responsible for visiting and supervising the victims of cruelty or neglect. Nursing and private children's homes were to be registered and inspected. Children under 14 were banned from public houses and it became illegal to sell cigarettes to those under 16. The legal system was also reformed to establish Juvenile Courts and to separate children from adult criminals; this built on the 1907 decision to introduce Borstals (residential centres providing education) for young offenders. As with the earlier Education Acts, the 1908 Children's Act represented a significant extension of the role of the State in the welfare of children.

b) Poverty and the Elderly

The elderly man or woman, forced by poverty to live out his or her last years in the workhouse, was one of the most tragic images in literature at the turn of the century. However, this picture distorted reality because by the early 1900s most of the elderly relieved by the Poor Law were receiving outdoor relief, and even in the workhouses conditions were more relaxed. Nevertheless, the poverty of the elderly and the stigma of the Poor Law had provoked a generation of campaigners to look for alternative methods of helping the aged poor.

As early as 1878, Canon William Blackley had proposed a pension scheme based on the contributory principle: people would pay a regular weekly amount into a fund which would provide them with an income when they reached a certain age. Joseph Chamberlain took up the cause in the 1890s and in 1898 a Treasury committee reported in favour of contributory pensions. However, such a scheme faced two difficulties. Firstly, many of the poor would not be able to afford the contributions; that, after all, was why the poorest were, in effect, excluded from membership of friendly societies. Secondly, the friendly societies themselves were totally opposed to a contributory scheme, as it would represent competition for the limited savings of the working class. Governments were fearful of the political power of the friendly societies, so proposals for a contributory scheme made no headway.

An alternative scheme was put forward in the 1890s by campaigners led by Charles Booth. Booth believed in a non-contributory scheme: the elderly would receive pensions by right and the pensions would be financed through taxation. This was opposed by those, like the COS, who believed that thrift and self-help should be the only keys to unlock the door of poverty in old age. If pensions were available as a right, they asked, why should anyone bother to save for their later years? The second obstacle to non-contributory pensions was finance: the estimated cost in the 1890s was £16 million, more than the total expenditure on the Poor Law. Although a Select Committee of the House of Commons in 1899 recommended the introduction of non-contributory pensions, the drain on public finance caused by the Boer War destroyed this plan.

By 1908 there was a broad consensus in favour of some form of old age pension. The Labour Party and the TUC had supported the campaign for Booth's pension scheme which was led by F.H. Stead. The friendly societies had come to realise that the drain on their reserves caused by elderly members claiming sickness benefit could be stopped by the introduction of state pensions. They favoured a non-contributory scheme so that there would be no new competition for working-class savings. Even the COS now accepted the need for pensions, although only contributory pensions were acceptable because of their self-help principles. H.H. Asquith, the Liberal Chancellor of the Exchequer, had begun to investigate the possibility of state pensions in 1906, and in April 1907 the cabinet agreed to a non-contributory scheme, which they introduced the following year.

The 1908 Old Age Pensions Act was brought in by David Lloyd George, who had succeeded Asquith as Chancellor. A non-contributory pension of 5 shillings per week was to be paid to everyone over 70 who had an income of less than 8 shillings per week from other sources. Those with incomes of more than 8 shillings were to receive a reduced pension on a sliding scale. Those with an income of more than 12 shillings per week got nothing. Anyone who had been imprisoned in the previous ten years, or who had claimed poor relief in the last two, or who was a drunk, or who had habitually failed to find work, was also excluded.

There is no doubt that the old age pension was popular. The government had estimated that there would be some 500,000 pensioners, at a cost of £6.5 million, and were surprised that 650,000 actually claimed the pension in 1909, at a cost of £8 million. By 1915, the number of pensioners had risen to just under one million. By paying pensions through post offices the government succeeded in completely divorcing them from the Poor Law, thus revealing, in the words of Lloyd George, 'a mass of poverty and destitution which is too proud to wear the badge of pauperism'.

The payment of pensions as of right, removing the Poor Law stigma

Some of the first elderly people to collect their old age pensions from the Post Office

from a welfare benefit, and the decision to finance a non-contributory scheme out of general taxation, can be seen as new departures in the way the State responded to poverty. On the other hand, it is possible to view the introduction of old age pensions as less than radical. Firstly, the age at which the pension became available was very high. The setting of the age at 70 was harsh for people in their 60s who could no longer earn a living. Secondly, the amount itself was very meagre. 5s. per week was only sufficient to top up an income. It was hardly enough to survive on by itself. Indeed, Churchill admitted that the government had, 'not pretended to carry the toiler to dry land. What we have done is to strap a lifebelt around him'. In fact, the government has been charged with changing little more than the name of the benefit. The proportion of pensioners claiming the pension in 1909 was similar to the proportion claiming Poor Law relief before the Act. Moreover, the usual weekly Poor Law payment in the early years of the century was around 5s. - the same as the pension. This has led Eric Midwinter to describe old age pensions as, 'in practice, the "nationalisation" of outdoor relief for poor people … the scheme demonstrated little more than a transfer from local to central taxation.'[3] Thirdly, a continuing belief in nineteenth century morality was betrayed by the removal of ex-offenders and the 'workshy' from those eligible for pensions. The notion of the 'deserving' and the 'undeserving' had not gone away. Pat Thane called the new benefit 'a pension for the very poor, the very respectable and the very old.'[4]

c) Poverty Due to Low Wages

In the nineteenth century governments had passed a number of factory acts dealing with issues such as child employment, hours of work and safety. However, the idea that they would legislate to set minimum wages was an intervention too far. The widespread faith in the operation of the free market held that wage rates could only be set by the laws of supply and demand. It was thought that any attempt by the State to interfere would cause bankruptcy for the firm concerned and unemployment for the workers. Yet Booth and Rowntree had both revealed that one of the major causes of poverty was the inadequacy of wages and this could not be ignored. In particular, conditions in the so called 'sweated' trades had been revealed as scandalous following a long campaign. The report of the 1908 Select Committee on Home Work described the problem well:

1 … if 'sweating' is understood to mean that work is paid for at a rate which, in the conditions under which many of the workers do it, yields to them an income which is quite insufficient to enable an adult person to obtain anything like proper food, clothing, and house accommodation,
5 there is no doubt that sweating does prevail extensively. We have had quite sufficient evidence to convince us (indeed it is almost common

knowledge) that the earnings of a large number of people - mainly women who work in their homes - are so small as alone to be insufficient to sustain life in the most meagre manner, even when they toil hard
10 for extremely long hours. The consequence is that, when those earnings are their sole source of income, the conditions under which they live are often not only crowded and insanitary, but altogether pitiable and distressing.

The result of such concerns was that the government did decide to intervene in the setting of some wages. The 1909 Trade Boards Act established minimum wages for 200,000 workers in the box-making, tailoring and lace-making industries. The minimum rates, both for those who were paid by the hour and those who were paid according

THE SWEATER'S FURNACE: OR, THE REAL "CURSE" OF LABOUR.

Punch attacks sweating, 1888

to their output ('piece' rates), were to be set by Boards made up of employers' representatives, workers' representatives and civil servants. The government also intervened to set minimum wage levels for miners by the 1912 Mines Act. Though limited in scope and in effect, these measures did mark a significant shift away from the nineteenth-century *laissez faire* attitude that the government should not intervene in the setting of wages.

d) Poverty as a Result of Illness

One of the greatest fears in all human societies is the fear of ill health. In turn of the century Britain, despite the public health reforms of the nineteenth century, death rates remained high. This was particularly the case in poor areas. The infant mortality rate, which is regarded as a particularly sensitive measure of public health, had remained at 153 per 1000 and showed little sign of reducing.

The concern about 'national efficiency' meant that the Liberals were well aware of these problems. Between 6 and 7 million people had some form of medical insurance in the early 1900s. However, many people found it difficult to keep up regular payments and let their policies lapse. Poor people who could not afford to insure themselves through friendly societies faced a grave crisis when the need arose to seek medical attention. This was compounded by the loss of income which would result from the illness of a wage earner. Lloyd George and his New Liberal colleagues decided that their priority was not illness itself, but the poverty that resulted from illness. As he explained to an audience in Kennington in 1911,

1 So long as the head of the family is in good health, on the whole with a
   fierce struggle he can keep the wolves of hunger in the vast majority of
   cases from the door; but when he breaks down in health, his children
   are at the mercy of these fierce ravaging beasts, and there is no one to
5 stand at the door to fight for the young. What happens in these cases?
   In hundreds of thousands there is penury, privation, everything going
   from the household, nothing left unpawned, except its pride.

The cost of old age pensions convinced the Liberals that they would be unable to finance health protection directly from taxation. Lloyd George had visited Germany and been impressed with their social insurance scheme. Thus the Liberals decided to deal with the problem of poverty caused by ill health through a system of compulsory health insurance.

Even more than was the case with pensions, there were powerful vested interests in the way of any national health insurance plan. The medical profession, though anxious to escape from the contracts imposed on many doctors by the friendly societies, did not want to become state employees. The friendly societies themselves knew that a government insurance scheme would all but destroy the reason for their existence. The large commercial insurance companies such as the Prudential were worried about the profits they would loose as a result of state competition. Employers campaigned against both the cost and the time that any scheme would involve for them. Many workers themselves objected to the idea of compulsory deductions from their wages. Mindful of the experience of the workhouses, they were also wary of any extension of state interference in their lives.

Part One of the 1911 National Insurance Act attempted to reach a compromise which would satisfy this opposition. The administration of the scheme would be carried out by friendly societies, trade unions or commercial insurance companies approved by the government. The cost of insurance was to be divided between the parties involved: male workers would pay 4d. per week into the insurance fund (3d. for females), their employer 3d. and the State 2d. In return, the insured worker would be entitled to free medical treatment by a doctor chosen from a panel organised by the local insurance commission. Men would also be entitled to 10s. per week sick pay (7s.6d. for women) for the first 26 weeks of sickness; women would receive 30s. maternity benefit; a disablement benefit of 5s. per week was to be established, and sufferers from tuberculosis and certain other diseases would be entitled to free treatment in a sanatorium or other specialist institution. Insurance was to be compulsory for all workers between 16 and 70 earning under £160 per year. Employers would be required to deduct the worker's contribution from his or her wages and to purchase special stamps to the value of the contributions which would be stuck on the worker's insurance card.

Out of all the Liberal welfare reforms, National Health Insurance was the most ambitious, the most important, and, probably, the most unpopular. The fact that workers were forced to contribute led to resentment. Although Lloyd George attempted to promote insurance by claiming that workers were getting '9d. for 4d.', poorer employees found that their wages had, in effect, been cut. Moreover, because everyone paid the same contribution regardless of income, the poorest workers lost the highest proportion of their earnings. The Webbs described the worker's contribution as a poll tax and argued that the scheme should have been funded by an extra tax on the rich. Nevertheless, despite these criticisms, by 1914 about 13 million workers were insured under the scheme. An important safety net for the alleviation of poverty caused by ill health had been established.

e) Poverty as a Result of Unemployment

Two years into their administration, the Liberal government was confronted with an unemployment crisis. By 1908, 7.2 per cent of the workforce, or 800,000 people, were out of work. Booth and Rowntree had already identified unemployment as an important cause of poverty, and now the Liberals were forced to do something about it.

The human misery that resulted from unemployment can be glimpsed through the reminiscences of people like Louise Santer. Born in 1894, near Hastings in Kent, she remembered the unemployment of her father, who was a scaffolder,

1   I can remember my father walking to Crowhurst in the snow drifts
     trying to get to work. There was nothing in them days ... If you hadn't
     got work you got nothing. Us children, we often got no bread ...
     Sometimes we couldn't go to school because if it was wet we got no
5   shoes. We must have owed the baker and the grocer some money.
     They used to let us have credit, but we never could pay them.

The nineteenth-century reaction to unemployment had often been to blame the individual for his failure to find work and to deny that the State could do anything about the problem. If workers failed to help themselves the only alternatives were charity or the Poor Law. By 1908, attitudes had begun to change, and the new thinking on unemployment was spelled out by William Beveridge in his book *Unemployment: A Problem of Industry*, published in 1909. Beveridge had been sub-warden at the Toynbee Hall settlement in East London from 1903 to 1907, where he had been influenced by Charles Booth. In 1908 Beveridge joined the Board of Trade as a civil servant and his views were an important influence on the Liberals. Beveridge believed that unemployment was an inevitable result of the capitalist industrial system. He said that there were bound to be periods of depression when work could not be found, no matter how hard an individual looked for it. Rather than blame the individual, Beveridge believed that workers needed help to locate the work that was available and financial support if they still could not find employment. He also believed that the State could do something to create work in times of depression. These three elements were to form the basis of Liberal policy on unemployment.

The 1909 Labour Exchanges Act was intended to promote the mobility of labour: in other words, to help the unemployed find the work that was available. In an age of limited communications, such an initiative was intended to relieve some of the hardship experienced by people like George Barnes. Barnes moved to London having worked in the shipyards of Barrow-in-Furness. He described his search for employment:

1   I faced the winter as one of London's unemployed. And then began for
     me the hardest struggle of my life, a real struggle for existence ... I had
     to get work, and I laid myself out to get it. But it was a weary job ...
     From my lodgings in Sadlers Wells I have set out day after day with no
5   better guidance than the advertisements in the *Clerkenwell News*, subse-
     quently expanded into the *Daily Chronicle* - which was the best adver-
     tising medium of the London dailies. I acquired a knowledge of London

which, like Sam Weller's, was extensive and peculiar, for I knew every engineering workshop from Thorneycroft's of Chiswick to Vicker's of
10 Erith.... That was the condition of things in my unemployed days.

Under the Act, men like George Barnes would be able to go to a local Labour Exchange and be advised of the vacancies in their particular trade. In order to encourage the unemployed to use them, both Beveridge and Churchill, the President of the Board of Trade, were keen to stress that the Labour Exchanges were separate and distinct from the Poor Law. Eighty-three exchanges were opened in February 1910 and there were 430 by 1914. In that year 2 million workers registered at the exchanges, which were finding 3,000 jobs a day. But the Labour Exchanges were not a complete success. Three-quarters of those registered did not find new jobs through the exchanges. Trade unions also remained suspicious of the Exchanges, believing that they were being used by employers as a way of lowering wage rates.

The second element in the Liberal answer to unemployment was a scheme to provide maintenance to those out of work. The Poor Law was no longer considered an appropriate way to deal with the unemployed and friendly society or trade union insurance schemes had failed to attract more than a minority of workers. The Liberals' solution was to establish a national unemployment insurance scheme incorporated in the same 1911 Act which introduced health insurance. The proposal was not to cover the whole workforce but just those trades which were particularly prone to seasonal or cyclical unemployment. Unemployment insurance was made compulsory for around 2.25 million workers in the building and construction, ironfounding, shipbuilding, mechanical engineering, vehicle construction and sawmilling industries. Employees had to pay 2.5d per week into the insurance fund and this was matched by 2.5d from their employer. The State contributed around 1.66d per week for each worker. Benefit of 7s. per week was available to unemployed members of the scheme, and contributors were entitled to one week's benefit for every five contributions paid, up to a maximum of 15 weeks. Subsidies were also made available to support trade union insurance schemes which paid higher levels of benefit.

As with health insurance, the contributory nature of the unemployment scheme was attacked on the grounds of unfairness: a flat rate contribution represented a higher proportion of a poor worker's income than that of someone who was better paid. To counter opposition to contributory benefits, Churchill had argued that the contribution principle was essential because it would establish that workers had a right to benefit and would at last remove issues of morality and blame from support for the unemployed. 'I do not like mixing up morality and mathematics', he said, and argued that those who contributed had a right to benefit even if they had lost their job deliberately. In fact, Churchill was overruled on this matter and the 1911

Act stated that anyone 'who loses employment through misconduct or who voluntarily leaves his employment without just cause' would be excluded from benefit. The scheme was only intended as a first step and it only covered a minority of workers. Some two-thirds of those insured in 1913 were skilled workers and this indicates that the scheme did little for the really poor. Nevertheless, between July 1913 and July 1914, 23 per cent of insured workers claimed benefit and this shows that unemployment insurance was meeting a need. The scheme marked another decisive break from the Poor Law treatment of unemployment and established the principle that maintenance of the unemployed was a responsibility of national government rather than a local matter.

The third element in the Liberal response to unemployment was an attempt to create work in times of depression. Local job creation schemes had been a response to unemployment since the 1886 Chamberlain Circular and the 1905 Unemployed Workmen Act had empowered Distress Committees to provide temporary relief work. The Liberal plan was to create a Development Fund which would stimulate employment through public works in time of depression. The fund, which was set up in 1909, also worked by promoting local initiatives, and in this sense it could be seen as a continuation of previous policies. However, the attempt by central government to intervene in the economic cycle was a radical break from nineteenth-century attitudes. For the next 70 years British governments were to accept that intervention to promote employment was both possible and necessary.

4 The Origins of the Welfare State?

> **KEY ISSUE** Can the Liberal social reforms be regarded as the origins of the welfare state?

Many historians have described the Liberal social reforms as representing the origins of the welfare state. Derek Fraser in *The Evolution of the Welfare State* highlights National Insurance in particular as representing 'the origins of the welfare state', and he concludes his chapter on Liberal social policy by asserting that, 'whatever historical perspective is used, one cannot escape the conclusion that Liberal social policy before the First World War was at once at variance with the past and an anticipation of radical changes in the future.'[5]

The term 'welfare state' is commonly understood to mean the system of social welfare established by the Labour governments of 1945-1951. The key elements of this system were a comprehensive range of benefits to compensate for loss of earnings due to unemployment, old age, sickness or widowhood; free and universal health care and education; and central government responsibility for the promotion of full employment and a healthy environment. It is clear that many of these elements echoed the initiatives of the Liberals before 1914: benefits outside the Poor Law were established and the Government began to accept the need for central action to deal with unemployment. Moreover, the man whose report provided the inspiration for the establishment of the welfare state in 1945, William Beveridge, was a key figure behind the Liberal reforms of 1908-14. In order to finance their reforms, Lloyd George made a significant attack on the rich in his 1909 'People's Budget'. The 1945 Labour government also sought to redistribute wealth from the rich to the poor through high taxes and high levels of public spending.

On the other hand, there were significant differences between the Liberal measures before the First World War and the Labour measures after the Second World War. The Liberals came to office without an overall strategy for the relief of poverty, and many of their reforms were little more than responses to pressing economic and political circumstances. Victorian moral attitudes were present in all the reforms, the financial value of benefits was limited, and many of the poor found that they remained outside the unemployment insurance net. The fact that health and unemployment insurance both relied on workers' own contributions was a significant difference from the 'cradle to grave' support offered in 1945, even if National Insurance did continue in the welfare state.

Nevertheless, despite the lack of an overall plan, despite the persistence of some Victorian morality, and despite their limitations, it is probably fair to say that the Liberal reforms provided at least some of the foundations of the welfare state. Attitudes to poverty and welfare had undergone a fundamental shift.

References

1   Simon Lemieux, *A Rogue Result: Liberal Landslide 1906 in Modern History Review* (November 1992), p. 17.
2   Discussed in Keith Laybourne, *The Evolution of British Social Policy and the Welfare State* (Keele University Press, 1995), p. 133.
3   Eric Midwinter, *The Development of Social Welfare in Britain* (Open University Press, 1994), p. 76.
4   Pat Thane, *Foundations of the Welfare State* (Longman, 1982), p. 83.
5   Derek Fraser, *The Evolution of the Welfare State* (Macmillan, 1973), pp. 175-176.

Working on Chapter 6

There are two key elements to this chapter. Firstly, make a list of the reasons for the Liberal social reforms. Secondly, make a list of the reforms themselves. For each reform you will need to note five things: the background to the specific reform; the reform itself; the positive effects of the reform; the weaknesses of the reform, and the ways in which the reform did or did not mark a break from past attitudes to welfare. The diagram below provides a brief summary of these points:

Summary Diagram
The Liberal Social Reforms 1906-14

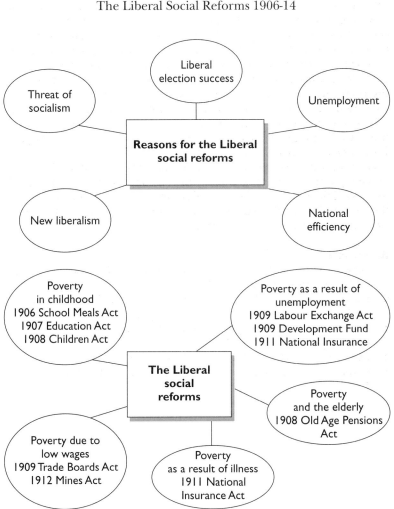

Answering structured and essay questions on Chapter 6

Essay questions on the Liberal social reforms tend to focus on either the causes of the reforms or the nature of the reforms. It is important that you distinguish between the two. A question on the causes of the Liberal social reforms, particularly if it is the first part of a two part structured question, may ask:

'Why did the Liberals introduce so many social reforms in the period 1906-14?'

In order to answer this question, you will need to outline each of the possible explanations for the Liberal social reforms. You will need to give some indication of how strong each of the possible explanations is. In your conclusion you should point to the explanation(s) which you believe to be most credible, on the basis of the evidence you have read.

Questions may suggest, particularly in the second part of a structured two-part exercise, that one of the background factors is the most important cause eg:

'The Liberal social reforms were motivated primarily by a fear of Labour'. Discuss.

This question demands that you first examine the proposal that the reforms were motivated by a fear of Labour. Why might the Liberals have feared Labour? Why might they have thought that social reforms would help them in their political struggle with Labour? Is there any evidence that this concern did motivate the Liberals? The second part of your essay should concentrate on the other factors which motivated the Liberals to pass social reforms. Outline these factors. How much evidence is there to suggest that they were prominent in the considerations of the Liberals. Try to look for clear evidence, for example what leading Liberals actually said. In your conclusion you must weigh up both sides of the argument. Because of the key word 'primarily' in the title, you must come to a clear conclusion - you can't just sit on the fence! Even if you believe that all the factors had a part to play, you must identify the cause(s) which had primary importance.

An essay question which concentrates on effects might be like this:

How far did the Liberal social reforms represent a break with Victorian attitudes to poverty?

After writing an introduction which explains how you intend to answer the question, you must include a paragraph outlining what you consider to be the essential Victorian attitudes to poverty. The rest of your essay should then consist of two parts. Firstly, outline the ways in which the reforms can be considered a continuation of Victorian attitudes. Secondly, outline the ways in which they can be considered a new departure. An alternative strategy is to deal with each reform in turn, outlining the two sides of each. Be careful that you do not get diverted into describing the reform rather than analysing it. Whichever approach you use, conclude with a paragraph which evaluates the arguments and comes to a clear judgement.

Source-based questions on Chapter 6

1. The reasons for state intervention
Read the extracts from Winston Churchill on page 99, J.M. Roberts on page 100, Herbert Gladstone on page 101 and the Inter-Departmental Committee on page 102.

a) Explain Churchill's reference to a 'slice of Bismarckianism'. (2 marks)
b) What did the Inter-Departmental Committee mean by 'ameliorative and arrestive measures'? (2 marks)
c) To what extent are the four extracts in agreement on the reasons for state intervention? (6 marks)

2. School Meals
Read the extracts on pages 102 and 105.

a) Why were Sir Arthur Clay and Helen Bosanquet opposed to free school meals? (2 marks)
b) To what extent would Sir Arthur Clay and Helen Bosanquet have agreed with the conclusions of the Inter-Departmental Committee on Physical Deterioration? (4 marks)
c) In what ways did the decision to introduce school meals mark a turning point in the provision of state welfare? (4 marks)

3. Sweated labour
Look at the cartoon on page 110 and the extract on pages 109-110.

a) In what ways does the cartoonist attempt to influence his audience on the issue of sweated labour? (4 marks)
b) In what ways did the 1908 Select Committee on Home Work criticise 'sweating'? (4 marks)
c) To what extent did the 1909 Trade Boards Act deal with the criticisms made in the cartoon and the Select Committee report? (7 marks)

7 Conclusion: Change and Continuity

POINTS TO CONSIDER

This final chapter draws together some of the major themes in the book. You should form your own opinion about how far there had been significant changes in the extent of poverty and the provision of welfare in this period. You also need to evaluate the arguments about the extent to which the foundations of the welfare state had been laid before 1914. Finally, you need to compare and contrast the different schools of historical thought on this subject. How convincing do you find them?

KEY DATES

1834-1929 Period of the New Poor Law
1906-14 Period of the Liberal welfare reforms
1945-51 Establishment of the 'welfare state' by the Labour government

1 What had Changed?

KEY ISSUES What changes were there during the period in the amount of money being spent on the poor? In what ways had attitudes to poverty changed? How far had poverty been reduced in this period?

In 1909 Lloyd George brought in the 'People's Budget' which increased taxes on the rich in order to pay for welfare measures. At first sight, this suggests that expenditure on the poor had increased by the end of this period, and the statistics bear this out. In 1831 total expenditure on poor relief in England and Wales was £7,037,000 for a total population of 13.9 million, an expenditure per head of just over 10 shillings. The result of the New Poor Law was to reduce expenditure: only £4,761,000 was spent on the relief of the poor in 1841 despite the population rising to 15.9 million. Expenditure per head of population in 1841 had dropped to just 6 shillings. In fact, although Poor Law spending fluctuated throughout the century, spending per head never again reached the pre-1834 levels, although it had risen to over 8 shillings per head in the years before the First World War. However, the £15 million being spent on the Poor Law in 1911 was doubled by government expenditure on old age pensions, National Insurance and the other liberal social measures. Not only had state spending on the poor increased, both in total and per head, but the

Year	Population (millions)	Total Poor Law Expenditure (£ millions)	Poor Law Expenditure per head	Government Spending on Old Age Pensions & National Insurance (£ millions)
		Welfare Expenditure in England and Wales 1831-1911'		
1831	13.9	7.037	10s 1d	0
1851	17.9	4.963	5s 6d	0
1871	22.7	7.887	6s 11d	0
1891	29.0	8.643	6s 0d	0
1911	36.0	15.023	8s 4d	9.800

amount of welfare produced by charities, friendly societies and trade unions had also clearly increased.

In some ways the growth of spending on welfare at the end of the period mirrored a change in the way that society looked at the poor, even if some attitudes remained the same. The writings of social investigators, like Charles Booth and Seebohm Rowntree, had shocked many with their revelations of the extent of poverty. Even groups committed to individualism, like the Charity Organisation Society, came to accept that poverty was more than just a matter of individual moral failure. If poverty was often caused by forces beyond the control of the individual, so it followed that the victims of these forces should not be treated as if they were guilty of a crime. The fundamental principle of the New Poor Law had been to stigmatise paupers, the implication being that they were to blame for their situation. Clearly the new attitudes meant that the New Poor Law was no longer an appropriate way to deal with the poor. Thus, all the social reforms of the Edwardian period sought to provide welfare outside the Poor Law and on terms which did not seek to humiliate and stigmatise the poor. The decision to pay old age pensions through post offices was the clearest statement that attitudes had changed; where once the elderly had been discouraged from claiming welfare, now they were positively encouraged.

Despite the attempts to treat poverty in a more sympathetic way, it is clear that the level of poverty had diminished little by 1914. The surveys at the end of the nineteenth century suggested that around a third of the population were living in poverty, with 10 per cent living in 'primary' or 'absolute' poverty (insufficient income for the maintenance of mere physical efficiency). However, in some respects, conditions for working people were better than they had been in the 1830s: legislation on factory conditions, public health and education had provided some protection against exploitation, disease and ignorance; 13-year-old children in state schools between 1900 and 1910 weighed on average 6.5 pounds more than children working in factories in the 1820s. The second half of the nineteenth century had also witnessed a significant rise in real wages for the working class as a whole. Certainly the fall in the death rate was a reflection that conditions had improved, although mortality rates continued to demonstrate the relative poverty of the working class. In 1911, infant mortality amongst the middle and upper classes was 76.4 per 1000 but 132.5 per 1000 amongst wage-earners. In a similar way, Oxbridge undergraduates in 1914 were on average taller and heavier than working class army conscripts in the 1914-18 War. The social reforms of the prewar Liberal government had no opportunity to make a major dent in the extent of poverty before the Great War, but there is some evidence to suggest that they (and the legislation of the 1920s which developed from them) began to make a difference in the longer term. When Rowntree conducted a follow-up survey in the 1930s, he found that the percentage living in 'primary poverty' had fallen from 9.9 per cent to 3.9 per cent. Considering that the survey was conducted in the depths of the 1930s depression, this does indicate a noticeable improvement. Rowntree himself acknowledged this progress, even though the same survey showed that a further 20 per cent continued to experience 'secondary' poverty.

2 Points of Continuity

> **KEY ISSUES** How far did poverty remain the most important reality in the lives of many working people? Did the provision of welfare at the end of the period retain many of the features of the Victorian era?

The reality of poverty remained as powerful in 1914 as it had been in 1830. Though average wages had risen and in many ways the world had changed, overcrowding, long working hours, insecurity, low wages and deprivation were still the experience of a large slice of the population. An even larger slice, probably the majority, lived with the fear that they might topple into this abyss. In her investigation into South London families just before the Great War, Maud Pember Reeves told this story:

1   A fish-fryer lost his job in Lambeth owing to the business being sold and the new owner bringing in his own fryer. The man had been getting 26s. a week and owed nothing. His wife's brothers and parents, who lived nearby, combined to feed three of the four children; a certain
5   amount of coal was sent in; the rent was allowed to stand over by a sympathetic landlady to whom the woman had been kind in her confinement; and, at last, after nine weeks, the man got work at Finsbury Park at 24s. a week. Nearly £3 was owing in rent, but otherwise there was no debt. The family stayed on in the same rooms, paying
10 3s. a week extra as back rent, and the man walked daily from south of

Kennington Park to Finsbury Park and back. He started at five in the morning, arrived at eight, and worked till noon, when he had four hours off and a meal. He was allowed to lie down and sleep till 4 p.m. Then he worked again till 10 p.m., afterwards walking home, arriving there at 15 about one in the morning. A year of this life knocked him up, and he left his place at Finsbury Park to find one in Westminster at a still slightly lower wage. The back rent is long ago paid off, and the family, now with five children, is still in the same rooms, though in reduced circumstances. When questioned as to why he remained in Kennington instead of 20 moving after his work, the man pointed out that the back rent would seem almost impossible to pay off at a distance. Then there was no one who knew them at Finsbury, where, should misfortune overtake them again, instead of being helped through a period of unemployment, they would have nothing before them but the 'house'.

Here was a man who worked hard and was clearly determined to lead a respectable life, yet the insecurity and low wages of his work brought him to the brink of distress. It is significant that the support of family and neighbours was considered the first resort in time of need. This was, and continued to be, the most important way in which welfare was provided. The State's welfare provision in the shape of the Poor Law, for this man and many others, continued to be a last resort. Paupers constituted only 2.5 per cent of the total population in 1911, although a further 500,000 workers were in receipt of National Insurance benefit by 1914 and nearly a million elderly people were claiming the pension. This means that even after the Liberal social reforms, only 6 to 7 per cent of the population were receiving state benefits. As the proportion of the population who were living in poverty was much higher than this, the role of the State in the relief of poverty in 1914 clearly remained limited.

There are two reasons why state provision for the poor continued to be limited. Firstly, it is clear that the impact of 'less eligibility' had been profound. The New Poor Law was designed to deter people from looking to the State for welfare, and in this respect it had been effective. Generations of working-class people had been brought up to fear the workhouse, and the shame and humiliation that became attached to pauperism lingered on, even when welfare was provided outside the Poor Law. Even though the Liberals deliberately avoided the Poor Law when establishing their welfare systems, the Law itself was not abolished. The spectre of the workhouse continued to be a powerful symbol throughout the land. Despite a general relaxation in conditions, paupers in some 'casual' wards were still picking oakum in the 1920s. The Poor Law was not abolished until 1929 and, even then, it took a long time to transfer its responsibilities to other bodies. When the Second World War broke out in 1939, 149,000 people were still living in institutions under the Poor Law.

The second reason for low take-up of state welfare had to do with the nature of the Liberal social reforms themselves. The Poor Law, for all its faults, had been a universal system. Anyone in need could apply for help, even though they were discouraged from doing so. While old age pensions were more or less universal (certain categories were excluded: see pages 107-108), they were subject to a strict means test. An elderly person with a weekly income of over 12s. per week got nothing. National Insurance was limited by design. Health Insurance was provided for all manual workers, but not their families. The workers themselves could be excluded from the scheme if they were considered 'bad risks'. As late as 1938, National Health Insurance still only covered 42 per cent of the population. Unemployment Insurance was even more restrictive, with only workers in a limited number of trades participating in the scheme. Although the coverage for the unemployed was eventually extended, the insurance principle continued to restrict entitlement to benefits. Unlike the Poor Law which preceded them and the welfare state which followed them, the Liberal measures did not represented a coherent welfare system open to all.

3 Historical Interpretations of Poverty and Welfare Reform

> **KEY ISSUE** What are the different ways in which historians have interpreted the pattern of poverty and welfare in the nineteenth and twentieth centuries?

Historians are products of the age in which they live, and interpretations of this subject have developed as contemporary attitudes to poverty and welfare have developed. In the period after the Second World War, the welfare state (see pages 115-116) was established. Historical writing in the 1960s and 1970s reflected the public consensus in support of the welfare state at this time. Historians like D. Roberts (*The Victorian Origins of the British Welfare State*, 1960), B.B. Gilbert (*The Evolution of National Insurance in Great Britain: the Origins of the Welfare State*, 1966) and Derek Fraser (*The Evolution of the British Welfare State*, 1973) wrote books whose very titles proclaimed a line of development leading from the Poor Law and the Liberal social reforms to the welfare state of the later twentieth century. Such an interpretation has been criticised as a 'Whig' view of history. This is the school of historical thought which identifies lines of historical progress in the development of society. It is generally an optimistic view, which sees society's progress as a positive thing, each development building on its predecessor to create better social and institutional arrangements. In the view of these historians, society learnt from the mistakes of the Poor Law and the inadequacies of individualism and created a collectivist and universal welfare system which was much better than its predecessors. The support for the welfare state across the political spectrum in the period 1945-75 convinced these historians that their analysis was correct.

The collapse of the consensus in support of the welfare state in the last quarter of the twentieth century led to something of a re-appraisal. Fraser, in his postscript to the 1984 edition of *The Evolution of the British Welfare State*, acknowledged that things now looked rather different from the way they had seemed ten years earlier:

> 1 We can now perhaps trace, more clearly than would have been possible in 1973, the whole life cycle of the welfare idea. It germinated in the social thought of late Victorian liberalism, reached its infancy in the collectivism of pre- and post- Great War statism, matured in the univer-
> 5 salism of the 1940s and flowered in full bloom in the consensus and affluence of the 1950s and 1960s. By the 1980s it was in its decline, like the faded rose of autumn.[2]

The uncertainty about the future and value of the welfare state in the late twentieth century resulted in historians questioning the 'Whig' interpretation. If the welfare state was under threat, perhaps, they suggested, its coming about was not as inevitable and clearly sign-posted as had previously been thought. Historians in the 1980s and 1990s were, in any case, beginning to question the validity of grand explanations of historical development. These 'postmodernist' inter-pretations emphasised the untidy and discontinuous nature of history and stressed the importance of chance and accident in the develop-ment of social institutions. This type of analysis also allowed historians to concentrate on areas of history which had received little attention in the 'big' accounts of the development of poverty and welfare. For example, feminist historians began to examine the effect of welfare reforms on women, while others drew attention to the significance of women's informal family, friendship and neighbourhood networks in providing welfare in their own communities. In her book *Growing up Poor* (1996), Anna Davin has charted the history of children in poor communities in the period 1870-1914, a hitherto neglected subject.[3]

Another response to the contemporary 'crisis' of the welfare state has been a conservative reaction against the welfare state. This view stresses the positive elements in the Victorian approach to poverty and sees the seeds of late twentieth-century problems in the abandon-ment of these Victorian values. Gertrude Himmelfarb, in *The Idea of Poverty* (1984) and *Poverty and Compassion* (1991), is perhaps the best example of this approach.[4] Professor Himmelfarb, particularly in her 1991 work, attempts to rescue the late-Victorian middle classes from their critics by emphasising the value of morality in addressing the problems of poverty. She highlights the widespread Victorian view, held, she claims, by the working classes as well as the middle class, that individual moral responsibility was the key factor in improving the lives of the poor. Other historians had charted the transition from a moralistic view of welfare provision, sorting the deserving from the undeserving, to an objective view, dealing with categories of need, as representing social progress. Himmelfarb takes the opposite view and implies that the abandonment of morality, as a central element in welfare policy, has been a prime cause of the failure of the modern welfare state.

While conservatives like Himmelfarb argue that the State went too far in the direction of welfare provision for all, left-wing interpretations have stressed the inadequacy of welfare and the persistence of poverty. Marxist and left-wing interpretations of poverty and welfare have traditionally emphasised that both are reflections of the class structure of society. Poverty, according to this view, is an inevitable consequence of capitalism. For example, unemployment is something that suits capitalists because it helps to keep wages at a lower level than they would be if everyone had a job. Employers can always tell their workers that if they do not accept their pay and conditions there will be someone out of work available to replace them.

Historians who have examined the provision of welfare from a Marxist perspective have generally taken the view that neither philanthropists nor the State genuinely want to get rid of poverty. Both are reflections of the class system and are interested only in preserving capitalism. Welfare, according to this perspective, is only provided as a concession to workers, in order to keep their loyalty to a system against which they would otherwise rebel. As Eric Hobsbawm wrote in *Industry and Empire* (1968):

1   ... whenever crises threatened to become unmanageable, the penalties of allowing them to get out of hand were always present in the minds of the country's rulers. There has hardly been a moment when the politically decisive section of them forgot the fundamental political fact of
5   modern Britain, namely that this country could not and cannot be run in flat defiance of its working-class majority, and that it could always afford the modest cost of conciliating a crucial section of this majority.[5]

This conciliation took the form of different welfare responses in different periods. For example, while observers like Thomas Malthus had argued for the complete abolition of the Poor Laws, politicians in the 1830s realised that without some provision for the poor there might be a revolution. In a similar way, leading Liberals like Churchill were quite explicit in their hope that welfare measures would discourage voters from looking towards socialist alternatives.

Marxist historiography hit something of a crisis in the late twentieth century. Marxism's prediction, that capitalism would eventually collapse and be replaced by a socialist system run for the benefit of the workers, suffered a major blow with the collapse of the East European communist states in the late 1980s and early 1990s. Communist China also began to embrace capitalism. Even left-wing historians, who had seen these totalitarian states as distortions of true socialism, were shocked by the failure of socialist politics in Western

Europe and the triumph of free-market capitalism under leaders like Margaret Thatcher. Marxists of an older generation, like E.P. Thompson and Eric Hobsbawm, continued to defend their interpretations, but few historians in the last decades of the twentieth century were prepared to develop their ideas in a convincing way.[6] Nevertheless, as we have seen, contemporary attitudes have an important influence on historical perspective. A crisis of capitalism and a resurgence of left-wing politics could lead to a revival of the view that poverty might yet be abolished as society finds a better way to run its affairs.

References

1   Karel Williams, *From Pauperism to Poverty* (Routledge & Kegan Paul, 1981), Statistical Appendix, pp. 145-235.
2   Derek Fraser, *The Evolution of the British Welfare State* (Macmillan, 1984 ed.) p. 253.
3   Anna Davin, *Growing Up Poor* (Rivers Oram, 1996).
4   G. Himmelfarb, *The Idea of Poverty* (Vintage, 1984); *Poverty and Compassion* (Vintage, 1992).
5   Eric Hobsbawm, *Industry and Empire* (Pelican, 1969) p. 17.
6   Hobsbawm, ibid.; E.P. Thompson, *The Making of the English Working Class* (Pantheon, 1964); Paul Johnson, *Class Law in Victorian England* (Past and Present, Nov. 1993).

Working on Chapter 7

This chapter attempts to do two things. Firstly, it indicates what had changed in terms of poverty and welfare by 1914, and what had not. Secondly, it examines the different interpretations that historians have constructed when studying this subject. One way to make notes on this chapter would be to list all the ways in which attitudes to poverty, welfare provision and the level of poverty had changed by 1914. Then make another list of the ways in which things did not change. Come to your own conclusion about the extent of change. You also need to make short summaries of the key interpretations of the subject. The diagram on page 128 should help with your note-making.

Answering structured and essay questions on Chapter 7

Questions which ask you to survey change over a long period may be of two types. The more straightforward type of question will ask you to explain the changes that have taken place. eg:

1. What were the major changes that took place in attitudes to poverty and welfare between 1834 and 1914?
2. How did the role of the State in the provision of welfare change in the period 1834-14?

Summary Diagram
Conclusion - Change and Continuity

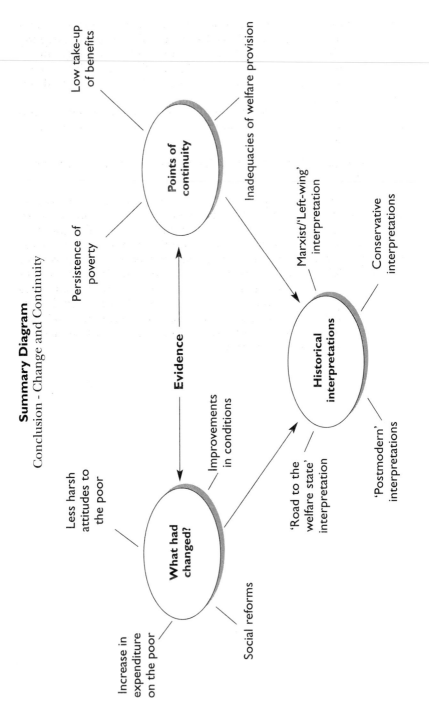

Both questions require you to compile a list of the most important changes. Each key change will need a paragraph to explain. Keep the key word '*change*' at the forefront of your thinking throughout. In your concluding paragraph you should assess the relative importance of the changes and make a judgement about which one you think was most significant.

The more complex type of question will involve an analysis of two sides of an argument - the familiar 'To what extent …' or 'How far …' type questions eg:

3. To what extent had welfare provision for the poor improved significantly by 1914?

As always with this type of question, you must be analytical. Describing the improvements is not, by itself, enough. You need an introduction which outlines how you intend to answer the question. Then the main body of your answer should be split into two parts. Firstly, you need to outline and explain the ways in which welfare provision *did* improve significantly. Secondly, outline the ways in which it *did not* improve significantly. Use material from your notes on this chapter to compile each set of points. In your conclusion, evaluate the two arguments and decide the extent of significant improvement. The word *significant* is important, and you will need to explain how you assess significance.

Further Reading

There are a large number of books and articles dealing with both poverty and welfare in general and the specific topics dealt with in each chapter. The brief survey below is not intended as a comprehensive review of this literature. However, it should give you a route into the more accessible texts which have been used in the production of this book.

1 Primary Sources

There are a number of collections of documents relating to welfare policy and practice in this period. As the titles suggest, Michael Rose, *The English Poor Law 1780-1930* (David & Charles, 1971) concentrates on the workhouse system. Eric Evans, *Social Policy 1830-1914* (Routledge & Kegan Paul, 1978) deals with a broader range of social issues and is particularly useful on the late Victorian changes and the Liberal social reforms. S.G. and E.O.A. Checkland (eds), *The Poor Law Report of 1834* (Penguin, 1974) provides the essence of an important historical document and is worth dipping into while Henry Mayhew, *London Labour and the London Poor* (Penguin Classics, 1985) remains a fascinating read.

The majority of the population who suffered from poverty in this period left little in the way of written evidence, so many of the accessible primary sources are written by middle-class commentators and reformers. Many of Charles Dickens' novels provide important insights into nineteenth-century attitudes towards poverty, as do the works of other authors such as George Elliot, *Middlemarch* (Penguin, 1965). Robert Tressell's novel, *The Ragged Trousered Philanthropists* (Grafton Books, 1965), provides an avowedly socialist interpretation which gives a powerful sense of the realities of working life at the turn of the century. Also from a left-wing perspective Maud Pember Reeves, *Round about a Pound a Week* (Virago ed. 1979) and Jack London, *People of the Abyss* (Panther, 1963), provide vivid, first hand accounts of life amongst the London poor before the Great War. Both are written by social investigators whereas Robert Roberts, *The Classic Slum, Salford Life in the First Quarter of the Century* (Penguin 1990), covers similar ground but is written by someone who grew up poor in the area he describes.

2 Secondary Sources

There are a number of readable overviews of the development of welfare policy from the Poor Law to the twentieth-century welfare state from an institutional perspective. Derek Fraser, *The Evolution of the British Welfare State* (Macmillan, 1973), is a standard text which has good chapters on the Poor Law, philanthropy and charity and the

Liberal reforms. Keith Laybourne, *The Evolution of British Social Policy and the Welfare State* (Keele University Press, 1995), Eric Midwinter, *The Development of Social Welfare in Britain* (Open University Press, 1994), and Pat Thane, *Foundations of the Welfare State* (Longman, 1982), though stressing different elements, all trace the antecedents of modern provision in nineteenth and early twentieth-century developments. Gertrude Himmelfarb, *The Idea of Poverty* (Vintage, 1984), *Poverty and Compassion* (Vintage, 1992), provides two volumes of immense scholarship which emphasise the importance of ideas and notions of morality in the shaping of social policy. For a conservative view which disputes the inevitability or desirability of the growth of universal state welfare they are well worth reading.

The Poor Law has attracted the interest of many historians and the literature on the Poor Law is vast. J.D. Marshall, *The Old Poor Law 1795-1834* (Macmillan, 1968), provides a good short account of the pre-1834 system whilst Anthony Brundage, *The Making of the New Poor Law 1832-39* (Hutchinson, 1978), traces the process by which the 1834 Act was passed. Michael Rose, *The Relief of Poverty 1834-1914* (Macmillan, 1972), in the 'Studies in Economic and Social History' series remains a useful short overview of the New Poor Law. M.A. Crowther, *The Workhouse System* (Methuen, 1981), is a more detailed analysis of the workhouse as an institution. Norman Longmate, *The Workhouse* (Temple Smith, 1974), is a less analytical but very readable account.

Accessible work on charity and philanthropy is less plentiful. Simon Fowler, *'Draining the bog': Charities and the poor in the nineteenth century* (Modern History Review, April 1998), is a useful starting point and there are useful chapters in Himmelfarb's *Poverty and Compassion* mentioned earlier. F.K. Prochaska, *The Voluntary Impulse* (London, 1988), and his essay *Philanthropy* in F.M.L. Thompson (ed.), *Cambridge Social History of Britain 1750-1950*, Vol. 3 (Cambridge, 1993), Chapter 7, provides a positive view of the role of charity whilst Robert Humphreys, *Sin, Organized Charity and the Poor Law in Victorian Britain* (St. Martin's Press, 1995), takes a very critical stance on the activities of the COS.

Two excellent recent works by historians who look at poverty from the perspective of the poor are Anna Davin, *Growing Up Poor* (Rivers Oram, 1996), and Carl Chinn, *Poverty amidst Prosperity* (Manchester, 1995). Eric Hopkins, *Working Class Self-Help* (UCL Press, 1995), gives a comprehensive introductory account of the activities of working-class institutions such as the friendly societies.

There have been few accessible recent works on the Liberal social reforms. J.R. Hay, *The Origins of the Liberal Welfare Reforms* (Macmillan, 1975), is a good starting point. G.R. Searle, *The Liberal Party, Triumph and Disintegration 1886-1929* (Macmillan, 1992), provides a political context for the reforms whilst B.B. Gilbert, *The Evolution of National Insurance in Great Britain: the origins of the welfare state* (Gregg Revivals ed., 1993), is still the standard work on perhaps the most important of the Liberal measures.

Acknowledgements

I would like to thank the series editor, Keith Randell, for his constructive criticisms throughout the process of writing this book. I am grateful to my colleagues and students at Richmond upon Thames College for their support, suggestions and encouragement. Thanks also to Dr Alan Clinton for his comments and advice. Most of all I would like to thank Gill Lawton for her patience and support which has been much appreciated.

Index

A selection of bestselling and related titles from Hodder & Stoughton *Educational*

Title	Author	ISBN	Price (UK)	
Labour and Reform:				
Working Class Movements 1815-1914	Clive Behagg	0 340 52930 X	£6.75	☐
The Growth of Democracy in Britain	Annette Mayer	0 340 69792 X	£6.75	☐
Poverty and Welfare	Peter Murray	0 340 61891 4	£6.75	☐
Chartism	Harry Browne	0 340 72070 0	£6.75	☐

All Hodder & Stoughton *Educational* books are available at your local bookshop, or can be ordered direct from the publisher. Just tick the titles you would like and complete the details below. Prices and availability are subject to change without prior notice.

Buy four books from the selection above and get free postage and packaging. Just send a cheque or postal order made payable to *Bookpoint Limited* to the value of the total cover price of four books. This should be sent to: Hodder & Stoughton *Educational*, 39 Milton Park, Abingdon, Oxon OX14 4TD, UK. EMail address: orders@bookpoint.co.uk. Alternatively, if you wish to buy fewer than four books, the following postage and packaging costs apply:

UK & BFPO: £4.30 for one book; £6.30 for two books; £8.30 for three books. Overseas and Eire: £4.80 for one book; £7.10 for 2 or 3 books (surface mail).

If you would like to pay by credit card, our centre team would be delighted to take your order by telephone. Our direct line (44) 01235 400414 (lines open 9.00am - 6.00pm, Monday to Saturday, with a 24 hour answering service). Alternatively you can send a fax to (44) 01235 400454.

Title _____ First name _____ Surname _____

Address _____

_____

_____

Postcode _____ Daytime telephone no._____

If you would prefer to pay by credit card, please complete:

Please debit my Master Card / Access / Diner's Card / American Express (delete as applicable)

Card number _____

Expiry date _____ Signature _____

If you would not like to receive further information on our products, please tick the box ☐.